# Poems From A Spiritual Heart

# Table of Contents

From the Darkness
A Glimmering Light
Lotus
The Lotus of Love
You Are OK
F.I.N.E
The Purge From Within
Purge Negativity
Scared
Silent Whisper
The In-Between
The Call of Prophecy
Darkness No Longer Dwells
Elimination of EGO
The Removal of Karma
Celestial Butterflies
Spirit Guide My Way
Call Home
I Make A Difference
The Difference I Make
I am Worthy
I Am
I Am All Various
I Am All There Is
We Are One

Together
Together United
I See Your Light
Full Moon
The Faith Inside
Journey Within
Let it Go
Touch The Sky
Diamonds in The Sky
Sapphire Night
My Wish
I Wish For All
You're Unstoppable
Unstoppable Joy
The Songs of Love
The Song of Goddess
Find Yourself
New Beginnings
It's My Time
I Will Shine
Open Up
Open Mind
Creating New Doors
Creating New Pathways
This is Your Song

Believe
Unity
Peace Within
Off World Beings
Wings Guide Me
Invoke Grace
Dancing Barefoot
Medicine Wheel
Animal Totems
Age of Obsession
Age of Oppression

## *Welcome Dear One*

Awaken now, oh dear one, arise from
slumber deep,
The sun adorns the sky, it's promise to
keep.
To dance within the sunrise, a rhapsody so
pure,
Of love's eternal song, steadfast and
secure.
Harvest fields of wisdom in the garden of
your soul,
Allow life's many lessons to illuminate,
console.
Strum the chords of existence in your
celestial play,
Unveil the sacred mysteries of the Divine's
display.
Embrace the silver moonlight, under its
sacred glow,
For in its softest whispers, the secrets of life
you'll know.
Imbibe in the celestial stream, sip the nectar
of grace,

Ever flowing from the cosmos, reflecting in your face.
Feel the wind's caress, as it brushes past your skin,
Know it's a message from the cosmos, stirring deep within.
From stardust we are birthed, and to stardust we return,
Our spirits forever free, as universe's lanterns burn.
So navigate the realm of dreams, across time's endless sea,
A cosmic traveller you are, embracing eternity.
For within each fleeting moment, the eternal exists,
In every breath you draw, the divine persistently insists.
You are more than flesh and bone, you're the cosmos come alive,
Every cell within you sings, the Universe's cosmic jive.
You are spirit and stardust, intertwined with cosmic light,

Forever evolving, ascending to magnificent heights.
Welcome, dear one, to this grand cosmic dance,
For every step you take, ignites a divine romance.
This symphony of existence, plays just for you,
Each note resounds within, in hues of celestial blue.
For you are love incarnate, divine energy flowing free,
A conscious being of light, existing to simply be.
To love, to laugh, to learn, as time slowly unfurls,
Welcome, dear one, to this grand stage, called our World.

## *Oceanic Breath*

Beneath the luminescent blue of the vast
ocean,
Lie the hidden secrets of perpetual motion,
From morning twilight to night's lullaby,
Its powerful heart never dies.
There's an insistent pulse that ebbs and
flows,
With an incessant hush only the deep
knows,
Every undulation, every rolling crest,
Is the ocean's laboring chest.
It inhales and exhales with titanic breath,
Unfaltering, constant, no trace of death,
A seemingly quiet act of resurrection,
With every single contraction.
A tender intake, a ripple of life begins,
Unleashing forces deep within,
An escalation, the swirling surf,
A testament to the sea's rebirth.
It washes ashore in the lap of tides,
Erasing traces, old grudges hides,
With every gulp, every released sigh,
Comes the whisper of a new sunrise.

Inhale, exhale, expand, compress,
A tale of nature's boundlessness,
The ocean's voice, resonant and wild,
Echoes in every wind-kissed child.
It's the rhythm that spins the world around,
In the roar of waves, there's wisdom to be found,
With every oceanic breath we're taking,
Is a tale of the earth that's ever in the making.
In the cradle of the sea's tender chest,
Life blooms anew in perpetual jest,
The continual cycle, inhale and escalation,
Reside in the heart of every creation.

# Ocean's Chorus

Life flows in rhythm, a grand, cyclic orchestration
With the ocean's endless pulse as an eternal validation
Of nature's resilience, embracing a systematic iteration,
A constant inhale and escalation in harmonious continuation.
Just as the ocean, relentless and in a tranquil state,
Expands its realm, defying both limits and fate,
We too find rhythm in cycles, infinite and innate,
A life's drama set to nature's intimate pulsating rate.
From ebbing tides to a raging storm's thrust,
There lies a myriad of mysteries in the ocean's robust,
Mirroring life's vicissitudes, unfair and just,
Ever fluid, yet always a silent custodian of trust.
Each swell, a tale of struggle and assertion,

Every crest, a peak of dreams in
continuation,
And every fall, an humble touch of
abnegation,
Unveiling truths in cyclical motion without
cessation.
From the azure depth rises the phoenix in
all her grandeur,
An offering to the celestial, exalting in
candid fervour,
Marking a poetic rhythm, infinite and of
measured composure,
The inhale and escalation of life, an oceanic
exposure.
As we voyage on life's undulating sea,
seemingly constant,
Tugged by forces known and unseen, our
progress relentless,
We comprehend our place in this cycle, so
vast and abundant,
Riding on waves of time, encapsulated in
moments that are current.
So, listen to the ocean's chorus, enduring
and gracious,

Reflect upon life's ceaseless cycle, potent and vivacious,
Feel the incessant flow, tumultuous, tranquil and audacious,
And rise, thrive, in the inhale and escalation, spectacularly spacious.

# Life's Grand Stage

Upon life's grand stage we've all been cast,
From diverse paths, together amassed.
Each one of us playing a unique role,
Separate acts that shape a collective soul.
We're doctors, teachers, artists, dreamers,
Bankers, builders, chefs, redeemers.
Different scripts, distinct parts to play,
But bound by the theater of everyday.
The costumes we wear, the masks we hold,
Tell a tale, poignant and bold.
Varied threads of human emotion,
Boundless as the farthest ocean.
We laugh, we cry, we hope, we fear,
Expressing what we hold dear.
Different paths, separate pursuits,
But together we form the play's attributes.
Despite our distinct roles and acts,
Inextricably, life's plot connects.
Shared hopes, collective dreams,
Form the seams of humanity's streams.
We are dancers in a cosmic ballet,
Shifting and turning, night and day.

Separately skilled, together sublime,
Playing our parts in the pantomime of time.
For the roles we assume, the acts we do,
Reflect that we're a similar crew.
Every actor, every stage hand,
Part of a tapestry, intricate and grand.
Upon life's grand stage we unite,
With different roles to ignite.
Separate stars in the endless night,
But together, we radiate light.
So remember, as your role unfolds,
We're all part of the same grand play's
molds.
Diverse we stand, together we connect,
On the stage of life, as a perfect project.

# No Judgment

Beyond the veil of earthly divide,
No judgment waits, in love we confide.
Loved ones long passed, no grievances
keep,
In celestial spaces, where time doesn't
seep.
Not confined by frailty or bias of man,
Freed of the fetters that mortality can,
Just an awareness, a knowing divine,
The connection is eternal, forever benign.
Like whispers of wind, in autumn leaves
sigh,
In echoes of truth, no secrets belie,
Where love is the language, understanding
the guide,
No shadows of judgment, in their light, we
confide.
Through time, through space, beyond mortal
sight,
Rekindled in stars, in ethereal light.
A bond of affection that cannot erase,
Love ones echo still, in celestial embrace.
Just love remains, and love alone,

In the silent symphony of the cosmic unknown,
For they speak a language not of reproach,
But of forgiveness, and love beyond approach.
An orchestra of stars sing their song,
Where hearts are united, where we all belong.
In an echo of time, no falsehoods deny,
No judgment, just love, beneath an endless sky.
So when sorrow weaves threads through your weary heart,
Remember their love, ever shall not depart.
Through the fabric of cosmos, beyond mortal plight,
There's no judgment, only love from the other side's light.

## *Universe's Light*

In each heart a universe dwells,
Life's sacred secrets in whispering cells.
Our pulse is rhythm, is celestial rhyme,
Unveiling the mystic dance of time.
A mote of cosmic dust we may be,
In an endless expanse of celestial sea.
Yet within each heart, a star is born,
A radiant echo of creation's morn.
Silent carriers of universe's light,
In tiny vessels, hidden from sight,
We hold galaxies in DNA's spiral strands,
The universe, a part of us, in our hands.
We gather the whispers of wind and flame,
Decode the language of stars in the name.
Each experience a verse, each knowledge a
sonnet,
In the ceaseless exchange, life spins its
sonnet.
We tread gently on time's fragile crest,
Holding its essence within our breast,
In this ocean of existence, where we unfold,
We are the story the universe has told.
Stardust imbued with living fire,

Sculpted by dreams and molded by desire,
Bearing love's wisdom in every iota,
Insignificant and yet, a miracle quota.
Borne of cosmic consciousness divine,
Reflecting galaxies in soul's design,
The boundless wisdom in each spirit's
fusion,
Echoes of eternity, life's grand illusion.
For we are but droplets in the cosmic flow,
Holding secrets that galaxies know,
Our essence interweaves the universe's
fabric,
Each life a verse, profound and magic.
Yes, each of us, a unique constellation,
Mapping out existence's vast sensation,
Seemingly insignificant in our strife,
Yet in us breathes, the boundless life.

# *I Am Here*

If I were to plant roots deep in this place,
In the silence and spaces between echoed
breath,
Would it resemble a blossoming face,
Or feel akin to a quiet dance with death?
Mornings born under cerulean hues,
Whispered lullabies from the emerald trees,
Night, like a silken shroud of muted blues,
Amid the company of shadow and breeze.
Days marked by rhythm, patterned and
planned,
Would contentment dare to show her
tranquil smile?
Basking in moments drawn in soft sands,
Captured like distant stars across many a
mile.
Yet, why am I here, treading unseen trails,
Chasing enigma dressed in life's guise?
I am here to unfurl the thousand tales,
Held captive in the deep, cavernous eyes.
To drink in laughter and shed healing tears,
To endure, to feel, to fathom the pain.
Embrace joy and parley with all my fears,

Until life and I, each other's reflections
remain.
Thus, I am here, for life is an echoing
rhyme,
A perpetual rhythm, a call we heed.
Beyond reason, transcending the hold of
time,
It's a heartfelt voyage in thoughts, words,
and deeds.

## NDE

In the cosmic array of celestial dust,
Where comets roam and stars combust,
There lie platforms silent, profound,
Broadcasting messages of truths unfound.
Born of galaxies, nebulae ablaze,
Where silence shouts and whispers praise,
Through cosmic winds, each echo hushed,
The universe tells stories in moments,
crushed.
Every twinkling star, a voice so dear,
Sings of mysteries that slowly clear,
Each astral streak, a vivid line,
In the epic tale of space and time.
Silhouettes against the cosmic tide,
Hold these messages, secrets inside,
Waiting in quietude, and with patience
immense,
To weave their story into our senses.
Astounding truths of aeons past,
Through echoes of light and shadows vast,
In the silent hymn of the cosmos sway,
Where ancient whispers never stray.
And so, we listen, we observe,

To the celestial tale, each curve,
While the universe speaks, quiet and
discreet,
On these platforms, where science and
mystique meet.
As dust particles to galaxies morph,
Therein, unfold life's beautiful worth,
Hidden in every speck of celestial flare,
The universe shares, for those who dare.
So, look above to the cosmic chart,
Feel the rhythm of every beating heart,
Each stellar whisper, each celestial dream,
For the universe talks, in silent streams.
Pay heed to these messages in flight,
Painted across the canvas of the night,
Remember, beneath the vast expanse of
skies,
The universe sings, speaks, sighs.

# *Cosmic Manuscript*

In cosmic swirls of dust and light,
Lie secret messages in starry night.
In the ether of infinite space,
An echo of universal embrace.
Across galaxies, they roam and float,
Unseen letters, an ethereal note.
Painted by quasars, stars, and comet,
A story told by a cosmic poet.
Sent through nebulae, on radiant beams,
Wrapped within quantum dreams.
Encoded in the pulsing heart,
Of nebula clouds and black holes dark.
Sometimes we catch a tiny whisper,
A celestial love letter or a soft whimper.
Echoes of creation's primal song,
Echoing through eons, oh so long.
Can you hear it, the celestial chant?
In starlight's silence, so distant, so
enchanting.
Open your heart, still your mind,
In every atom, wisdom you'll find.
This cosmic manuscript, oh so vast,
In every star, in light amassed,

Has messages from the divine,
A celestial scripture, endlessly intertwined.
Sometimes the universe uses these
platforms,
Transcendent stages, in myriad forms,
To share messages profound, incredible,
In its silence, wisdom inaudible.
Yet, in every soul, it does resonate,
In silent whispers, it does propagate.
In starlight's song, in comet's trail,
Are hidden messages, a cosmic tale.
A tale of creation, of stars and dust,
Of the infinite universe, in us thrust,
And so, my dear, let us listen,
To the universe's symphony, let us glisten.

## ♥ ~ *Eyes in the Darkness*

In the hallways of my mind, in the twilight of
my sleep,
I started seeing faces, all I did was weep.
I knew not their stories, knew not their woe,
I began to see their journeys, of people I
didn't know.
Whispers and echoes of cries unheard,
Faces marked with battle, tales undisturbed.
Within these contours, etched lines of hope,
A testament to resilience, an unwavering
scope.
They were waiting for me, in that silent
space,
Emerging from my despair, to face life's
embrace.
To find myself once more, through the
shadow and gloom,
And in their waiting faces, find the courage
to bloom.
Now these phantom images, these ethereal
parts,
Whisper in my dreams, pulsate in my heart.
If I surrendered, ceased to play my role,

Not only would I lose, I'd surrender my soul.
So I embraced the challenge, dared to
begin,
For my life had lessons, wrapped deep
within.
In this hall of faces, a mosaic of pain and
strife,
I learned to impart wisdom, found my
purpose in life.
For I saw not just strangers, in those distant
eyes,
But fragments of my story, mirrored in their
cries.
Their presence was a prayer, their pain a
sermon,
Each waiting face a reminder, each
struggle, a burden.
Every face that I meet, every eye that I
greet,
Bears the same hopeful glint, the same
quiet defeat.
But through the shared suffering, we learn
and we grow,
And that's the beauty of the story, the faces
bestow.

Each person is a verse, each heart a prayer,
We find each other's lessons in the lives we
bear.
In seeing and being seen, we find the
strength to teach,
And the gift in each waiting face, is the
wisdom we reach.

# The Power of Trusting

In the cosmic wheel of life and lore,
Spirit whispers a timeless score,
Underneath the vast night's dome,
Whispering secrets in hallowed tones.
Chasing wisdom from the Divine,
Down ancient paths, through tendrils of
time,
An age-old tale of trust and faith,
As tranquil as a river's wraith.
Trust in the Divine plan so grand,
Crafted by the cosmic hand,
Sculpted from the stardust of old,
Inscribed in the sacred spiritual mold.
Beneath the golden celestial sea,
Blossoms the eternal decree,
Beyond all vision and perception,
Lies the trust, the sacred connection.
Trust, O souls, in the divine decree,
In unseen wonders yet to be,
In the mystical chords of life's song,
In paths, untraveled and untrodden, yet
belong.
Trust, in the silence of the night,

In the hushed whispers of the light,
In the Spirit's guidance, so profound,
In the sacred truths, forever sound.
Fear not the tempest nor the wave,
For in trust, you are strong and brave,
Every twist and every turn,
Is a lesson the Spirit yearns you to learn.
For trust is the key that sets us free,
The beacon in the cosmic sea,
Trust in the Spirit, in the divine decree,
And witness the majesty of eternity.
Oh, what a wonder, what a sight,
To trust in the Spirit, in its infinite light,
One profound lesson for humanity,
The remarkable power of trust's divinity.

## *Co-Creation*

In the realm of eternal cosmos, we blend,
Creating an intertwining of energies without
end.
Your love, like radiant beams of ethereal
light,
Combined with my spirit, ignites the celestial
flight.
Burn so bright, our co-creation of existence,
A union of souls that resists worldly
resistance.
Through galaxies unexplored, we dance and
twirl,
In this realm, you and I, against the world.
With starlit sparks and the echo of divine
chants,
Together, we perform the universe's sacred
dance.
Through nebulae, constellations and planets
untamed,
The fire of our love eternally uncontained.
You and me, beneath the star-lit canopy,
A divine design of cosmic harmony.

Boundless and limitless as the heavens above,
This is our story, a co-creation of love.
Bathed in the radiance of love so divine,
To you, my beloved, my soul will ever align.
In each sacred moment, in each spiritual spree,
Together, in divinity, forever we will be.
A divine symphony we echo in this cosmic abyss,
Each celestial note, a testament of our bliss.
In the cosmic tapestry, our love will forever glow,
Together, we are divinity, creating love as we flow.
Through celestial fields of dreams, we fly,
Illuminating the cosmos with our ethereal sky.
So burn so bright, oh co-creation of light and love,
For together we embody the divinity from above.

## *Trust Your Spiritual Blueprint*

In the silhouettes of thoughts that drape,
In the quiet whispers that our hearts make,
A truth profound, in soul is etched,
A wisdom deep, in silence sketched.
A journey not meant for the mortal's grasp,
A cosmic play, in eternity's clasp,
Look not outside, seek not afar,
The answers lie where your questions are.
With eyes wide shut, and mind's door ajar,
Embark on a voyage to your inner star,
In shadows dark and labyrinths deep,
Lies a sacred pledge you're destined to
keep.
Trust not in voices that echo outside,
But the resonating chorus, inside you abide.
In moments quiet, listen and hush,
To the architect divine, within the soul's
crush.
Every sunlit dream, every teardrop's flow,
Every laughter's bell, every wind's blow,
Are brushstrokes subtle, on your life's
canvas vast,
Of the celestial artist, in the moment's cast.

Each heartbeat whispers a cosmic song,
In every right and in every wrong,
Look not outside, for within the muse,
Lies the blueprint, of the path you choose.
Let the heart decode, let the spirit unravel,
The sacred notes, on this inward travel,
For in the divine orchestration, soul's
tranquil play,
Trust in your blueprint, for it's the only way.
Remember, we're more than bodies wearing
a skin,
We're souls, perfecting lessons within,
To become the architect, who designs and
crafts,
Our own fate's ship, sailing infinite drafts.
Trust in your blueprint, let faith be your map,
In love's eternal flame, let your spirit
unwrap,
The masterstroke of destiny, in life's infinite
script,
Is not something created, but within us,
cryptic.
For we are the architects, shaping our
realm,

Guided by the Creator, with love at the helm,
The eternal truth whispers softly, My dear,
Trust in your blueprint, have no fear.

# *Love of the Heart*

In this space, so ethereal and vast,
From the heart, the love shall last,
Blooms of compassion, joy unfurled,
Sending ripples through the world.
Shrouded in the glow of celestial light,
On the canvas of soul, love takes flight,
Echoes of laughter, sounds so divine,
Fused with spirit, our essence intertwine.
Auroras of love, ethereal blooms,
Dancing through cosmos, it perpetually
looms,
Through depths of despair and heights of
elation,
Boundless, our hearts echo love's
vibrations.
In celestial harmonies, notes align,
Creating melodies, exquisitely divine,
And in the realm, where the spirits dance,
A symphony of love unfolds in a trance.
From soul to soul, the rhythm of love,
Painting skies, on wings of the dove,
A journey to joy, the beacon of light,
Guided by the compass of inner sight.

So much love, compassion and joy,
Bringing from the heart, none can destroy,
Bathing in its warmth, serenity takes flight,
Sailing through eternity, in love's endless
light.
Embrace the glow, the heavenly ray,
Let love guide you, never astray,
Savor the essence, the ethereal art,
Embrace the symphony, the love of the
heart.

# The Compass of Inner Sight

Upon this realm where matter molds,
In every heart, a compass holds,
A guiding light, that silent voice,
Guiding us to the higher choice.
Embedded deep within the soul,
The compass of the heart takes control.
Revealing paths once veiled in mystery,
Navigating life's winding history.
No lamp nor lantern could hold such light,
As the compass of inner sight.
Its needle points to the divine,
A beacon of truth in hearts entwined.
This compass leads not to lands untold,
But towards virtues of love and courage
bold,
To kindness, patience and gratitude's
abode,
Upon this eternal spiritual road.
Trust its bearing, the truth unfurls,
In this celestial map of pearls.
Not charted by hand, not wrought by strife,
But guided by the compass of life.
It signals when we've lost our way,

And whispers gently when we stray,
Drawing us back to love's embrace,
Reminding us of our rightful place.
An inner wisdom, old as time,
Resounding in a cosmic chime,
Its power unyielding, steady and true,
This compass resides in me and you.
For we are travelers, roaming free,
Explorers of the vast life's sea.
In our pursuit for truths unwritten,
The compass of our souls, is ever smitten.
The compass of inner sight,
Guides through darkness, towards the light.
Unseen, but felt in the silent prayer,
In love, in dreams, it's always there.
So listen close, and you will hear,
The whispers of the compass clear.
Fear not, dear traveler, in the endless night,
For you are guided by inner sight.

# *Letting Go*

In silence, I close my eyes, and breathe,
Fear looming, curiosity weaving its wreath.
I prepare my soul for the words you'd
convey,
And in apprehension, I await your way.
Listening, I surrender to the vastness of
your truth,
In the divine symphony, I find my roots.
Through every spoken line, a petal unfolds,
Gifting clarity, to the seeker who beholds.
Trepidation sweeps, whispering tales of
doubt,
Yet courage grips my heart, pushing fears
out.
I anticipate the divine knowledge that you'd
cast,
Unseen yet felt, as shadows of the past.
An ensemble of stars, humming your
wisdom aloud,
A revelation breaks forth, breaking the
cloud.
The melodious harmony echoes your name,

Awakening dormant sparks, into a living flame.
My heart rejoices, reveling in your presence,
An ancient echo reverberates in reverence.
Embracing your wisdom, letting go of the fright,
Dancing to the rhythm of the guiding light.
Joy blossoms in my being, from the depth of the soul,
In your ethereal essence, I find myself whole.
Your truth unfurls like a radiant sunrise,
Filling the chambers of my heart with pure delight.
Your words resonate with an overwhelming might,
Piercing the veil of darkness with their light.
Imbuing my existence with spiritual growth,
Embarking me on an enlightening, sacred oath.

# The Lighthouse

Guiding light of the endless sea,
Thou silent sentinel, we bow to thee,
From darkness's mouth, your beacon
peeps,
Whilst all around, the cruel sea sweeps.
Oh beacon of hope, in stormy weather,
Leading lost souls, bringing them hither,
A lighthouse standing tall and bright,
A reassuring glow in the depth of night.
On a rocky outcrop, you firmly stand,
Against tempest's wrath, a faithful hand,
Guarding sailors from the night,
You are the bringer of divine light.
Though the seas are fierce, and the night
sky dreary,
Your luminance soothes hearts grown
weary,
You guide our way with steadfast love,
Your guiding star from heaven above.
With every flash, your message clear,
Lost and wandering, need not fear,
The journey's tough, the road is long,
But in your light, we are strong.

Light the way, oh Lighthouse tall,
Answer to the lost one's call,
Glow in the gloom, shine through the blight,
Ever burning, ever bright.
You speak of peace amidst the squall,
Of hope in despair, you tell us all,
A story of faith, strength and might,
As we navigate through life's longest night.
Oh Lighthouse, stand resolute, never cease,
Through all of life's storms, guide us to
peace,
Across the vastness of this infinite sea,
Your light of love is humanity's key.

# Love is Humanity's Key

In the symphony of life, on Earth's
expansive stage,
Sits humanity, contemplating wisdom of the
sage.
Yet the highest knowledge, the purest and
most grand,
Is the silent, selfless language only the heart
understands.
No pen nor prose, no eloquent speech,
Can wholly grasp love's concept, so beyond
our reach.
Yet like an eager lighthouse guiding weary
souls at sea,
In every heart's core lies this truth: love is
humanity's key.
It transcends faith, creed, colour and race,
Envelopes our world with an elegant grace.
Sews the fabric of the cosmos, makes the
silence sing,
Makes an ordinary mortal heart feel like the
grandest king.
For in the noble dance of atoms, beneath
reality's veil,

In the ethereal, shimmering quantum realms where words fail,
Love reigns supreme, unbound, unseen, always serene,
Its divine power echoing through life's ever flowing stream.
When winds of adversity stir life's tumultuous sea,
In the hearts that bear love, fear shall cease to be.
Love is the lamp illuminating life's mysterious night,
With its invincible glow, each heart finds its light.
Our mortal bodies are temporary, they age, they decay,
Yet the love that courses within us is eternally at play.
For love is more than fleeting emotion or simplistic sentiment,
It's the underlying melody to our existence, it's heaven-sent.
From galaxies above to the atoms we cannot see,

In the cosmic dance of divinity, love is the
harmonizing key.
Love is the source, love is the course, the
eternal decree,
The cornerstone of existence, love is
humanity's key.
In each kind gesture, in every selfless act,
In each humble word of solace, love's
essence remains intact.
For we are born from love, return to love, by
love we are set free,
Yes, woven in the threads of life, love is
humanity's key.
So remember this, dear traveller, in
moments of despair,
When hope seems elusive, and burdens
hard to bear,
The key is always within reach, in our
shared humanity,
For boundless, beautiful, enduring love is
humanity's key.

## *The Ringing in My Ears*

The ringing in my ears,
Your songs I do hear
the ringing in my ears,
Thank you for your bells and chimes
I know that your spirit is near
Your words I do not hear
But your voice is strong
Guiding me with love and light
Showing me to do what's right
The rainbows in my head I know
Are the songs of love that you were to show
The gift from you to me
is plain to see
The ringing in my ears I hear
Your voice so very very clear
I listening to your song
I know you rejoice,
joyous words will come along
When I listen to your song

# *Hum in my Senses*

The hum in my senses,
Your melodies I perceive,
This hum in my senses,
Gratitude for your sweet-toned rhymes,
I sense your spiritual presence nearby.
Your utterances I fail to discern,
But your voice is resolute,
Guiding me with tenderness and
illumination,
Teaching me to choose the righteous path.
The spectral colors within my thoughts, I
understand,
Are the harmonies of love you wished to
display.
The endowment from you to me Is evident
for all to see.
The hum in my senses I discern,
Your voice so profoundly clear,
I tune in to your serenade,
I comprehend you exult,
Blissful lyrics will soon emerge
When I absorb your lyrical song.

## Rejoyce

Awaken to the daybreak of divine radiance,
On the terrain of existence, a reverberating
cadence,
Through mountains high and valleys low,
rejoice,
For in each heartbeat whispers the
Creator's voice.
Do not let sorrow enshroud the flame of the
soul,
Look beyond, and find faith's magnificent
console.
Do not wait for tomorrows, embrace today,
And allow your spirit in each moment to
sway.
Witness the wisdom within every teardrop,
Ponder not on loss, on blessings never stop.
Take refuge in love's timeless cocoon,
Celebrate, for you are an iridescent tune.
The sun rays pierce the canopy of the dark,
Illuminate the wilderness, ignite a spark.
Purge despair, from hope never desist,
Unveil the Creator's resplendent tryst.
Upon the horizon of the unseen, lay trust,

In the silence, converse with the cosmic
dust.
Surrender to the song that the Universe
sings,
Behold the miracle that every sunrise
brings.
Journey through life as a fearless voyager,
Crushing chains of the past, be your own
harbinger.
Your spirit soars in celestial splendor,
In your core reside power, strong and
tender.
Oh human, embrace your spiritual
sovereignty,
You are not just a mortal, but infinity.
Open your heart to the chorus of creation,
In this symphony of souls, rejoice and find
liberation.
Rejoice in the voyage of spiritual
illumination,
Enriched by love, in the grand scheme of
Creation.
Revel in the oneness, in the cosmic
cohesion,

Embrace every heartbeat with profound compassion.
So, let your heart flutter on wings of freedom,
Nourished by divine love in heaven's kingdom.
Remember, your essence is pure, your soul effervescent,
Rejoice, for in God's eyes, you are iridescent.

# The Colors of Love

In the vast panorama of creation,
Emotions weave colors in grandiose
orchestration,
Among the hues and shades,
Lie the various spectrums of love's trade.
Crimson for the ardor that enflames hearts,
Tinged with Scarlet for passions that start,
The purity of White whispering of truth,
Bonding souls in an eternal youth.
Blue of serenity and gentle ease,
Nurturing trust over worldly seas,
Burning Orange for fierce loyalty,
Beating as one, in spiritual royalty.
Vibrant Yellow sparks joy, delight,
Purity of affection in sparkling light,
Pinky Peach blushes innocent and shy,
In love's tender, soft sigh.
Vivid Green embodies life's force,
Growth, rebirth in love's divine course,
Black's depth absorbs all, relentless,
In its fold, love becomes boundless.
Indigo channels intuition,
Silent conversations in love's mansion,

Violet dawns the spirituality,
Engulfing love in mystic reality.
Gold speaks of a love so divine,
That withstands the tides of time,
And Silver, it threads a hope so bright,
For love to prosper in darkest night.
Love then, is not a mere emotion,
But a divine, cosmic explosion,
Dissolving egos, tearing apart lies,
To be the truth, the universe epitomizes.
In every pulsating beat, in every breath,
In each fiber of life, in every depth,
In the harmony of souls, in heart's delight,
Flows the Colors of Love, shimmering
bright.

# The Light of Love Is All Around

The light of love
From the darkness is found
It brings me hope
and so I am bound
Traveling at destiny
With the light of love
Right beside me
We dance and we sing
We show others
All around
How to find
The light of love
It's all around

*******


From the coldness of hate
A warmth emerges great
A spark that kindles faith
An eternal and steady gait
Embarking on life's wavy sea
With the light of love guiding me
We laugh, we weave tales

Showing those on other trails
How to unlock the love
That is everywhere to discover.
In every place, in every sight
Shines the light, so brilliantly bright
The light of love is all around
A symphony of joy in every sound.
The scent of flowers, the song of dove

In all, you can find, the light of love.

# *From the Darkness*

Depression lingers
sadness is here
darkness all around.
Is there really anything to fear
no one seems to care
as I flutter in the night.
My sorrows are mine
without delight,
What's that I see
in the distance of far off sight
A glimmering Light
is it for me
I do not know from where it came
Its new and different
Am I to blame
Maybe something to behold
So I go near nearing
it gets brighter
and maybe a little more clear
maybe an urge
of it calling me close
the darkness of sadness,
it's all around

except for that one little ray of hope,
to be found
it calls me and I come
finding the light,
finding love all around
the jitters come from this little Ray,
It seems to brighten my day.
I give Thanks for the small little beam,
and it grows and glows
With each passing day.
It seems to make my heart gleam.
Things might not be,
 as bad as they once seemed.
Not so bad after all,
I look around,
I think I'm kind of tall.
Though the darkness and despair,
It's still here and there.
but the light it calls me,
It beckons me near.
so I go towards,
and I cherish the thought,
it's the love of the heart.
I walk towards this joyous relight
Leaving behind the darkness and fright.

Love it encompass me,
oh, so grand.
It fills my heart,
every little strand.
I dance, and I sing,
on mountain top once more,
I think I've been here once before.
the darkness, it seems so far away,
The light has replaced it,
almost every day.
the gratitude I feel,
for embracing love,
I give thanks to the light above.
I do give to the light
Guiding my way
Appreciation of hope
This and every day
my heart dances
I see something new
the distance there
Is that someone else,
Is that someone who cares.
Someone I once new,
Coming out of the dark.
The light of love feels my heart,

As I summon others from the dark.
This joy is too great,
not to be found.
so I shall spread my light,
for others around.

# A Glimmering Light

Depression engulfs, sadness pervades,
a surrounding darkness all over.
Is there truly anything to be afraid of?
Nobody appears to notice as I flutter
through the gloom.
My burdens are uniquely mine,
devoid of any pleasure,
yet I notice, afar off,
a glimmer of Light.
Is it intended for me?
I am uncertain,
This light is foreign and different.
Maybe it's something worthy of attention,
as it gets nearer, brighter and more
insistent.
The pull is irresistible, calling me to move
closer.
Despite the darkness of my woes,
there's a glimmer of hope,
a lone ray piercing the night.
It calls to me and I respond,
finding the light, discovering love.
There's a trembling sensation,

stirred by this small ray.
It appears to lighten up my day.
Gratitude overflows for this small yet
growing beam,
making my heart gleam with hope.
Things might not be as grim as they seem.
As I look around, a feeling of upliftment is
present.
Though shadows of despair linger,
the light continues to beckon me.
So, I draw nearer,
cherishing the gentle pull of warmth and
love,
into its inviting radiance,
behind the despair and fear.
Love surrounds me,
a sensation so grand,
permeating every inch of my heart.
Dancing and singing on the mountaintop
once more,
I realize this is familiar territory.
The darkness now seems so distant.
The light is slowly taking its place,
gradually illuminating each new day.
I am grateful for embracing love,

for the guidance of the divine light from above.

My heart dances as I discover new relationships.

The love-light fills my heart

I extend the invitation to those in the darkness.

The joy is too magnificent to be kept hidden.

Thus, I shall share my light with others around me.

# *Lotus*

Beneath the shadows of suffering,
A solitary Lotus breathes in silence,
Its roots embrace the dark mud,
Its petals kiss the sky.
Darkness cocoons the lotus,
A space to cradle despair,
And within the sacred gloom,
Desire begins to flower.
The sacred Lotus of love unfurls,
Against the heavy air of anguish,
Braving the mire and sorrow,
In search of divine nourish.
The lotus blooms with humble hope,
Emerging from pain and loneliness,
Transforming despair into desire,
It glows with radiant readiness.
From the seed of struggle and pain,
Grows the flower of desire,
The lotus blooms amidst the gloom,
Ignited by internal fire.
The blossom reaches for the cosmos,
Resonating with sacred sound,
The scent of longing fills the air,

Spiritual wisdom is found.
Love has flowered from darkness,
The lotus of longing in bloom,
Guided by faith, the desire of hope,
Against adversity it looms.
The lotus of love open desire,
In the midst of suffering, it shines,
The symbol of rebirth, of passion,
From the mud, divine love it finds.

# The Lotus of Love

From the abyss it stirs,
A lone beacon of beauty and light,
Unfurling from darkness and desolation,
Its petals, pale as moonlight.
Lotus of love, radiant and divine,
Bloom within my heart, sublime.
Upon the stagnant waters, your face so bright,
Reflects my soul, in tranquil light.
Resilience encased within your grace,
The wisdom of patience, time, and space.
Sublime blossom in the nocturnal vast,
Ever constant, unswayed by the past.
Amidst the silt and silent shadows,
Echoes the anthem of the meadows,
Cry of the lotus, heard only by few,
Speaks of love, faithful and true.
On waters murky, yet so serene,
A vision of purity, oft unseen,
Reveal, oh Lotus, in your mystic bloom,
Hope that conquers darkest gloom.
Transcend the shadows, dance in the light,
Embrace your power, oh blossom of night.

From mud and mire, the lotus ascends,
Spiritual journey, where the earthly ends.
Guiding my heart through despair and pain,
Oh sacred Lotus, bloom once again.
Alone in the darkness, your love is my
shield,
With every heartbeat, your truth is revealed.
With every unfurling petal of white,
My spirit takes flight in the silence of night.
Solitary Lotus, a reflection of my soul,
Your presence within, makes me whole.
For you, dear Lotus, symbol of peace,
Your essence within, shall never cease.
And though in darkness, you silently thrive,
In my heart, the Lotus is forever alive.

## *You Are OK*

In the serenity of a tranquil lake,
A sacred lotus bloom awakes,
Awakens to the light of the divine,
Where tranquility and peace align.
Floating on the mirrored surface,
Seems like time holds no purpose,
Enthralling charm, you resonate,
Heartfelt bliss you cultivate.
Petal by petal you unfold,
In your heart, wisdom you hold.
The sludge of pain, anger, and grief,
Through you transforms, to relief.
Moonlight shines on your silken petals,
Guided by ancient ancestral vessels.
Pure as snow, a celestial charm,
Harboring peace, bringing no harm.
Against the murky depths of sorrow,
You bloom with grace, fear you borrow,
Blossom forth with faith anew,
Sharing love, your divine cue.
Life's battles you patiently withstand,
Grace and strength go hand in hand.
Your sacred heart of spiritual delight,

Radiates a heavenly, guiding light.
The struggles in life may push and sway,
Yet you remain unscathed, come what may.
Your existence whispers to all who dare,
To seek within, for love to share.
I've got you, the Universe vows,
Gently stirring beneath your bows.
Infinite peace within your wake,
The perfect reflection, on the quiet lake.
Within you, I see my truth unfurl,
A perfect union of love in this whirl,
Sacred Lotus, with your soul pure,
Your essence whispers,
You are OK, for sure.

# F.I.NE.

When I say that I am fine,
Look into my soul, divine,
Hidden truth, you'll surely find,
Echoes of a darker time.
Frustrated, by the trials I face,
Injustice served with a steady pace.
Ebbing patience in this space,
Longing for that tranquil grace.
Insecure, my fears enclosed,
Behind smiles and lies I've posed,
Broken, hurting, love deposed,
From my spirit, light is doused.
Neurotic thoughts that echo loud,
An endless maze, I'm tightly bound.
Struggling to find a fertile ground,
In silent whispers, my mind is drowned.
Emotional is my beaten heart,
A wounded bird, with feathers part.
Tattered wings, unable to start,
From sorrow's canvas, I am art.
When I say I am just fine,
Read between the echoing line,
Witness this life of mine,

As I strive for the divine.
Understanding can indeed unwind,
The F.I.N.E. of an afflicted mind,
Treat with care and be always kind,
We are more than what we're confined.
So next time, I claim I'm fine,
Do not take it as a sign,
Look deeper, beyond the brine,
Seek my truth, for it does shine.

# The Purge From Within

Beneath the starlit canvas high,
A spirit dances in the sky,
It spins and whirls in cosmic grace,
Across the vast and infinite space.
No earthly ties to bind or pull,
Its essence, pure, and plentiful.
Within each soul, this spirit lies,
In the silence, truth resides.
Emerging from the darkest night,
A lotus blooms, a wondrous sight.
A testament to will and strength,
A journey of unfathomable length.
Just as a lotus finds its bloom,
In muddy waters, amidst gloom.
So does our spirit rise above,
In darkness finds the light of love.
When thoughts cloud and create fear,
Let go, release, make it clear.
Purge the heart from suffering's toll,
Rekindle the divine spark in your soul.
Like the lotus, let us rise,
Echoing its gentle cries.
Surrender to the cosmic flow,

Allow your inner light to glow.
Rise from the murky depths below,
Let your love and compassion show.
Unfold your petals to the sun,
A new spiritual journey has begun.
Our lives, like the lotus, can ascend,
From the mud, a message we send,
With courage and with faith, begin,
To realize the light within.

# Purge Negativity

Banish the thoughts that tie you down,
Frown not upon the sun's new day.
Release the sorrow, break its crown,
Let all the shadowed fears give way.
Away, away with jaded scorn,
Criticizing each dawning morn.
Grasp instead the joy reborn,
Turn toward the light of hope's adorn.
Shatter, shatter chains of dread,
Create a space of peace instead.
Let dreams once buried, raise their head,
Drink from the wells of joy widespread.
Cease, oh cease the downward dive,
Each heartbeat calls, you're alive.
Turn, awaken, revive,
Purge negativity and thrive.
Shred the veil of looming fears,
Wipe away the crystal tears.
Lift your spirit, drown the jeers,
See a world where love coheres.
Thrive, oh thrive, with hearts ablaze,
Fill each moment with sun's gaze.
Laugh with mirth in vibrant haze,

Choose joy over somber days.
To purge negativity is a task,
One we didn't choose nor ask.
Yet the freedom it'll unmask,
Is a bounty in our grasp.
Stand tall, dispel the dark eclipse,
Hope is anchored to your lips.
Banish despair's tenuous grips,
Set sail on a journey of joyous trips.
Unfurl, unfurl, like the dawn's delight,
Become the beacon in the starless night.
Chase the wind, in spirits bright,
Purge negativity, embrace the light.

## *Scared*

Stir within your spirit, my child
Embrace your fear and curiosity wild
Energetic as the radiant sun,
Walk with caution but also with fun.
Tales of your heart, let them unfold
Let your soul narrate the tales untold
Within your spirit resides a powerful light
That can pierce the darkest night.
Of pure love and joy, you possess a
treasure trove,
Do not lock it away, let it flow, let it show
Reflect the pureness of your essence,
Stand grounded in your own existence.
Harness the power that's in your hand,
Channel the energy, let it expand.
Ignite the flame of your being with your love
And see the magic it can shove.
For you've seen the darkest hour,
Yet beheld the beauty of a blooming flower.
Dark and light, the two facets of life,
The saga of joy, pain, peace, and strife.
Don't shy away, there's more to be
revealed,

Like the splendid sun after the dark has
healed.
For your heart harbors tales worth a million
gold,
My dear child, let your stories be told.
Glimmer and twinkle, like stars in the night,
Bask in your own inner light.
Rebirth your hope, let it sing,
Bring forth the joyous song spring.
And in this song of love and peace,
May your spirit find release.
May you see the light that you abound,
And in it, let your soul resound.

## *Silent Whisper*

In the silent whispers of the wind,
In the soft glow of the moon,
Seek the depths of your inner spirit,
Like a lotus ready to bloom.
Fear not what others may see,
In the mirror of their own reality,
Be guided by the inner sun,
That sparks curiosity.
Nurture your essence, cherish your dreams,
You are more than you seem.
Radiate with the love and joy,
that springs from your inner stream.
The shadows have danced and left,
In your heart, light has found its nest.
Reveal the tales yet untold,
In your spirit's brave quest.
Your light flickers like a celestial flame,
Filling darkness with ethereal light,
Instilling hope in those around,
A lighthouse in the night.
With the harmony of a heavenly choir,
Your joyous song reverberates,
In the rhythm of love and peace,

A new dawn it awaits.
Let the lotus within you unfold,
In this sacred dance, be bold,
In the symphony of the universe,
Your spirit's story is told.

# The In-Between

In the hallowed space of in-between,
Neither hidden nor overtly seen,
There in that borderless threshold does
exist,
An ethereal reality, wrapped in the mist.
In between the somber night and brilliant
day,
Where shadowed doubts and radiant faith
lay,
Brimming with potential for creation's birth,
The borderless in-between, that joins the
earth.
In between the hushed whispers of the soul,
And worldly noise, striving to control,
There thrives a sanctuary, pure and
profound,
Where cosmic mysteries ceaselessly
abound.
In between the heartbeat of the cosmos and
mortal's throb,
Where love's strength has the power to rob
All triviality of terrestrial affairs,
And amplify the melody of cosmic prayers.

In between life's start and life's demise,
We unmask the eternal in the temporal's
disguise,
Residing in the shadow, holding heaven's
light,
There in the silence, before the birth of the
night.
The in-between, the bridge to the divine,
That interstice of the temporal and sublime,
Where each moment embodies eternity's
breath,
The ethereal sanctuary where souls take
breath.
In the timeless instant, in the wordless
prayer,
In the love that moves from heart to air,
There we meet our maker, there we touch
our birth,
There, in the hallowed space of the in-
between's berth.
Oh the in-between, a symphony profound,
Its notes: the silences where miracles are
found,
Its rhythm: the breath of creation's grace,
In its melody, we touch our sacred space.

# The Call of Prophecy

Through the whispers of the divine,
A sacred message, subtly aligned,
It hums and stirs within my mind,
This silent call of prophecy, softly twined.
In gentle breezes, it sways the trees,
Carried in rustling leaves, whispering tales
of the unseen.
A spiritual note echoes on nature's rim,
An encoded rhythm, a hymn's serene sim.
A subtle hint in the sunset's hue,
A mysterious design in the morning dew,
Every stroke of divinity's pen,
Imprints this silent prophecy, again and
again.
Across the heavens, among the stars,
Beneath the moon, a narrative that scars.
With twinkling hope and speckled truth,
Shining upon the roof of our universal booth.
Where sunlight filters through the hush of
trees,
And dances with the fluttering of the bees,
There too is written this prophetic tale,
Bounded not by mortal jail.

Unfettered by our world's pretence,
Beyond our mundane senses' fence,
It speaks not with thunderous roar,
But in silence profound, forevermore.
I do not ask whence comes the voice,
Nor question this call, not by choice,
The whisper resonates, piercing my soul,
Guiding me gently towards my destined
goal.
Unseen, yet perceived, its mysterious touch,
Transcends reason, becomes a crutch,
A constant echo in the corners of my heart,
This call of prophecy, divine art.
I close my eyes, let it permeate,
Every sinew, every state,
Until the prophecy becomes me,
And in its whispers,
I am set free.

## *Darkness No Longer Dwells*

Beneath the moon's soft shrouded glow,
And beyond the twinkling celestial show,
Once there lived a shivering soul,
In a void, neither whole, nor a part of the whole.
Caught in a storm, forgotten by day,
A casualty of life's tragic play,
Whence sunlight flickered, no warmth to beget,
Hollow whispers, dreams of regret.
But darkness, no longer shall it dwell,
For Hope came calling, its gentle spell.
From despair's tempest,
Love began to blossom,
Cracked open the heart, to create a chasm.
Through that crevice,
Light made its way,
Uplifting the spirit from a relentless fray,
Strummed chords of the divine, singing its lore,
Filled empty spaces, didn't dwell anymore.
Wings spread wide, no longer forlorn,
Released from shadows that had it torn.

Through Heaven's winds, now the soul flies,
Released from the Earth, reaching out to the skies.
Moon's mystic hymns now echo so sweet,
In tune with the heart, the rhythm complete.
A tale of rebirth, no longer to be foretold,
In love, in light, a soul grows bold.
So if you find your soul's skies bleak,
Know, even the mighty often grow weak,
Call upon Love, for it never denies,
Look for the Light, for it never lies.
Darkness, dear soul, no longer dwells,
For you're kissed by light, where the divine dwells.
Arise, take flight, in cosmic ballet,
Bask in Love's warmth, by night and by day.

# Elimination of EGO

As morning rays erase the night,
Dawn arrives, making all right.
One must aim to free the mind,
In EGO's trap, do not bind.
Ego's shadow cloaks our soul,
From universal energy's pull.
It weaves a thread of vain deceit,
Chasing mirages, in heat's defeat.
Walls of ego, opaque and strong,
Limit vision, distort our song.
Erase the walls, embrace the light,
See the universe, broad and bright.
On this journey, truth prevails,
Love transcends, never fails.
Compassion bridges the vast divide,
When ego's whim, we set aside.
In every heart, a flame does burn,
In selfless love, it takes a turn.
This ember warm, lights the way,
Burning EGO, into humble clay.
Our thoughts, like waves, crash and collide,
Under EGO's shadowy tide.
Let's sow the seeds of unity,
To harvest peace, in community.

Life's voyage needs no vanity's crew,
Ego's demise brings a view.
Just pure souls in symphony,
Celebrate life's eternal spree.
In the silence of the soul,
EGO meets its rightful toll.
A place of peace and harmony,
Where only love is currency.
With ego's veil, duly lifted,
To the cosmic flow, we're gifted.
Infinite light replaces pride,
Once ego's ghost has truly died.
This precious human life we've won,
Is not for ego's fleeting fun.
Through mindful actions, thoughts and word,
In compassion's call, be heard.
Strive to empty, fill with love,
Life's true lesson, from above.
Let ego fall, in surrender complete,
Only then, is life truly replete.
Ego's elimination is not defeat,
But victory of love, so sweet.
From dust to stars, let's evolve,
In selflessness, let's dissolve

## The Removal of Karma

Unseen chains, forged in unseen fires,
Linked together, strands of desires.
They bind and twine, entwining the soul,
In karma's dance, in a ruthless role.
Attachments bloom, like a cosmic weave,
Shadows they cast, delusions they
conceive.
Mired in action, engrossed in gain,
Lost in Maya, this worldly reign.
Yet, silence sings a seraph's hymn,
Echoes of wisdom, subtly dim.
Bathed in light, purged from strife,
In stillness found, the essence of life.
So strive to peel, the layers of karma,
Undo the bonds, release the drama.
Seek the source, of conscious intent,
Where life unfurls, without torment.
Engulfed in peace, engulfed in light,
When worldly pulls, lose their might.
Mortal limits, broken, release,
Into eternal dance of celestial peace.
Witness the blaze of spiritual fire,
Kindled in truth, devoid of desire.

As layers fall, in cosmic play,
One's pure Self emerges, like the break of day.
Renounce the fetters of a bygone era,
Immerse thyself, in Truth's serene river.
Know the essence, beyond the skin,
Realize thou art, akin to divine kin.
Seek solace in the inner shrine,
Eternal truth, eternally thine.
The removal of karma, a saint's delight,
Emerging unbound, into the divine light.

## Celestial Butterflies

Beyond the vale of human sight,
Flutter celestial butterflies,
Transcending mortal tethered plight,
In star-studded cosmic skies.
Their wings, aglow with purest light,
Patterned with sacred truths unknown,
Kaleidoscope in silent flight,
To where divinity is shown.
Oh, that we could in faith aspire,
To possess such a luminous guise,
Ignited with holy fire,
Dancing in the eternal skies.
Though tethered we are to this earth,
We house an immeasurable worth.
An eternal soul given birth,
In the cosmos before our earthly berth.
Our spirits too are made to soar,
Despite the shadows that we wear,
Not bound by time, forevermore,
Gilded with stardust, light and air.
Beyond this realm of sight and sound,
Our true selves lie in wait unbound.
A butterfly, celestial, profound,

In the fabric of the universe is wound.
So let us quiet the world's harsh roar,
Listen for the silent cosmic hymn,
Where celestial butterflies soar,
Beyond the universe's brim.
Let's find that silent space within,
A cocoon of peace amidst the din,
From which our own transformation begins,
To join the dance we were made to spin.
Like the celestial butterflies we see,
Unfurling beauty in the vast decree,
May we too embody what we were meant to be,
A spectacle of light, boundless and free.

# *Spirit Guide My Way*

In the mystic haze of the silent night,
Beside the moon's calm and gentle light.
I raise my voice to the eternal sky,
Invoking the Spirit Guide who does not lie.
Barefooted on the dewy grass,
I breathe in deep, to let time pass.
Guide of Wisdom, hear my plea,
Open my soul and set it free.
Eagle-eyed keeper of eternal light,
Be my shield, become my sight.
Your silent whispers fill my mind,
A compass true, I am inclined.
For many trials await on my path,
Guided through them by your wrath.
You speak not with a voice so loud,
But through symbols, through the cloud.
Like ancient elders who sought the way,
To you, dear spirit, I sincerely pray.
Let me not falter, nor step aside,
Be my sight, in you I confide.
Teach me, o spirit, let me comprehend,
To see the unseen, to apprehend.
You stir my heart with a silent voice,

You navigate my life, guide my choice.
Navigate my dreams with your light,
Teach me discernment, strengthen my
might.
Grant me courage, strength to persist,
On this journey that's enveloped in mist.
Bathed in the moonlight's silver sheen,
In tranquil solitude, by stars seen,
My prayer to you does ascend,
Spirit Guide, my confidant, my friend.
An eternity passes, a fleeting beat,
Upon my lips, your wisdom is sweet.
Under the sky's canvas of moon and stars,
You heal my wounds, you hide my scars.
Invisible to eyes, but felt in heart,
Dear Spirit Guide, never shall we part.
Through dark tunnels, under cosmic sway,
You're the lantern, lighting my way.

## Call Home

nto the vast unknown,
Where secrets are kept and whispers blown.
A beckoning light, a sacred stone,
In a far-off place, I once called home.
It lingers still, this untamed call,
Beyond the wild, beyond the sprawl.
Barefoot I stand, and heed its draw,
Like a quiet serenade at the edge of all.
Dusk-dipped clouds and silver trees,
Lead me onwards through the seas,
My journey mirrors Hercules,
But instead of conquest, I seek release.
Past the grumble of thunder, past the veil of
rain,
Past the limits of sight, where day wanes.
My heart dances with an inner flame,
Oh, how it echoes that unending refrain.
Homeward bound yet ever lost,
A ghostly ship in tempest tossed.
No force exists, at any cost,
Could make me ignore this echoed gloss.
Oh I long for the place that exists not here,
Past the comfort zone, past the fear.
Where forgotten songs echo so clear,

In a far-off place, once so near.
In pursuit of a home, ever in my sight,
Guided solely by inner light.
I navigate the lonely night,
To chase the call that lingers bright.
Oh, how it sings, that sweet unknown,
From distant hills, and polished stone.
I know not where the path has flown,
Only that it calls me home.

******* ******* ******* *******

Beyond the veil of stars and distant
galaxies,
In a realm untouched by hands of Time, You
reside.
Unfathomable divinity, omnipotent, wise and
wide,
To You, the author of life and its complex
symmetries, I confide.
Under Your grand cosmic canopy, all of
life's intricacies,
Each human heartbeat, each leaf's fall, to
Your rhythm, they coincide.

From earth's foundation, to the
mountaintops, where eagles glide,
All creation sings a symphony of divine
epiphanies.
In quiet moments, when words are
whispered into the ether,
Humble supplications cloaked in midnight's
sweet reprieve.
We call upon Your name, for You to hold, to
heal, to perceive,
Your love, the strongest force, forever and
aether.
A wayward soul, wandering in life's
unending maze,
Struggling under the weight of the world, I
falter, I flounder.
Yet, Your soft whispers echo through the
silence, louder,
Be still, know that I am God, You  reassure
amidst life's blaze.
This earthly dwelling, only temporary, our
true home lies beyond,
A place of boundless love, where angelic
melodies abound.

A heavenly dwelling, where peace and joy surround,
There, You beckon us with love profound.
From ashes, from dust, I emerged, set in motion by Your will,
From celestial silhouettes, down to earth's tiny hills.
In moments of stillness, in the depth of silence, a gentle thrill,
I feel Your touch, I hear Your call, Your voice quietly instill.
You're the loving artist behind life's great canvas, this beautiful play.
The gentle wind that lifts the sparrows on their way,
The whispering pines, the babbling brooks, they subtly convey,
Your sweet, eternal song that guides me when I stray.
Oh, divine creator, unto You my soul does yearn,
A celestial connection, to call home, I ardently yearn.
And so, in each moment, each step, each return,

To You, to that cosmic cradle, my spirit will turn.

# I Make A Difference

Upon this earthly sphere, in vast, profound
expanse,
I am not a random drop in an ocean's
glance.
For every gentle word spoken, for every
generous deed,
Leaves a mark of love; to plant a powerful
seed.
To every creature, I am a messenger of
peace,
To the struggling, I am a release,
To the burdened soul, a comfort in distress,
To the forgotten ones, I am a loving caress.
My heartbeats echo in a universe divine,
They paint a celestial design.
I, an instrument of compassion's song,
Where do I belong?
Not among stars or to the azure skies,
Not in ambitions towering high,
Not in pursuit of vanities or transient
desires,
But where the eternal flame of love inspires.
I am the silent whisper of hope in despair,

The soothing balm for wounds laid bare.
To the downcast eyes,
I am the rising sun,
With every kindness shown, a victory won.
My presence is not limited to my own skin,
It touches every heart, every kin.
Though my physical form may cease to exist,
In every life I've touched, I persist.
An agent of love, an artisan of peace,
An antidote to strife, allowing hate to decrease.
My impact, unseen but real, often undefinable,
Echoes across the universe, unconfined, undeniable.
With every act of love, the universe resounds,
In each compassionate word, a celestial sound.
With every shared smile, with every heart that I lift,
I etch my presence, I make a difference, I am a gift.
For every person has the capacity to bring,

A ripple of love, in the smallest of things.
So walk with compassion, love with no limits,
Create, inspire, uplift, with every minute.
Though life may seem fleeting, and death looms near,
Our essence is eternal, that much is clear.
And with each act of kindness, in love and peace we strive,
Our soul whispers gently, 'you make a difference, you're alive.'

# *The Difference I Make*

As I wake to another sunrise, before God's own gaze,
I ponder in silence on the difference I can make.
I walk upon the earth, with heaven in my heart,
With my spirit kindled brightly, my day I start.
Within my soul, there's a calling, soft and clear,
To heal the world with love, dispelling every fear.
In this immense universe, my existence seems small,
But, within the heart's realm, I stand very tall.
For each act of kindness is a note in heaven's song,
Each tender word a lyric, where all of us belong.
A hand reaching out in support, a smile, a loving embrace,

Reveal the divine within us, a mirror of Its grace.
The words I speak, can inspire or simply break,
The hearts I touch, can awaken or just shake.
But, each choice I make with love, in thought or in deed,
In another heart plants, a love-infused seed.
In the moments of despair, in the cries of pain,
In the eyes that have forgotten to dream again,
I hope my touch brings healing, my words be the balm,
That helps to rekindle, in them, life's healing calm.
From the dawn's early light to the quiet of the night,
In every soul, I meet, I leave a touch of light.
In their smile, I see, a reflection of my love,
Sent back to me, like an echo from above.
This difference I make, no matter how slight,
Creates ripples in eternity, dispersing the night.

It serves as a reminder, under God's watchful eyes,
Each act of love is seen, nothing ever dies.
So here I stand, a humble spark, igniting in the dark,
Pledging to myself, leaving my small mark.
In each moment I live, in every heart, I touch,
The difference I make, will, in love, matter so much.

# I am Worthy

In the cathedral of my soul,
I stand tall and fearless,
No sermons of inadequacy,
Can sway my heart, the endless,
I am, the reflection of divinity,
And in every heartbeat, I profess,
I am worthy.
I roam not in the wilderness,
Searching for value in mortal praises,
Within me is a gold mine,
Full of wisdom and sacred phases,
To unravel it layer by layer,
I tread the journey of inner discovery.
I seek not approval from others,
Their vision clouded by earthly frailty,
I lean into the cosmos within,
Immersed in celestial vitality,
Guided by the divine conductor,
I dance to the melody of self-love merrily.
Fearless am I in the face of darkness,
A single ray in the abyss is enough,
Fueled by the light of understanding,

My soul becomes diamond tough,
I stride forward in the night,
Illuminated by the starlight of self-belief,
bright and bluff.
For every trial is a pathway,
Leading to realms of spiritual maturity,
Every sorrow, a blessing concealed,
Invoking deeper sense of surety,
For my essence is shaped by the divine,
Cementing my stance,
I am worthy.
Though world's scales might judge and
falter,
The divine justice knows no perjury,
As an indispensable note in creation's
symphony,
I add to the cosmic harmony,
Sounding out in love and truth,
Boldly I declare,
I am worthy.
The tapestry of existence is threaded with
my light,
For I am an irreplaceable verse in the
universal story,
Poured from the divine chalice,

In all my complex simplicity and glory,
I affirm with every breath I draw,
In all spaces and in all journeys,
I am worthy.

# I Am

I am the light that sears the shadowed
plains,
From divine forge of star-seeded might,
Burning not with ego's insatiable flames,
But radiance of unclaimed, untamed right.
I am the river, persistent in course,
Carved deep in the canyons of time's
embrace,
Quenching parched hearts with truth's
primal source,
In fluid refrains, love's undying grace.
I am the tree rooted firm in the earth,
Lifted high in an ethereal quest,
Within whispering leaves, find the birth
Of moments savored, existence blessed.
I am the silence, echoing wide,
Echoes resonating within one's soul,
With breathless space where secrets reside,
Caged within, yet forever whole.
I am the prism of life's iridescence,
Spectrum of emotion's palette rare,
Feeling the pulse of resonant essence,
Strumming cosmic threads, essence bare.

I am the eternal seer and sage,
Scouring vast vistas of boundless mind,
Scripting wisdom on the infinite page,
Endless chapters of humankind.
I am the self, seeking beyond form,
Yet housed within a shell of earth and air,
An eternal spirit, ardently warm,
Journeying to awaken, to be aware.
In stillness I stand, at life's cosmic wheel,
Divine essence clothed in human veer,
In this sacred silence, I am made real,
In love, in loss, in laughter, in fear.
For I am all, and all is within me,
Boundless as sky, profound as sea,
Cloaked in mystery's lyrical decree,
I am, forever and eternally.

## *I Am All Various*

I am the vast sea,
The endless sky, the fertile earth,
The blossoming tree.
I am the humming bird,
Whispering words in the wind,
Stories unheard.
I am the tranquil moon,
Casting silver dreams over night,
Vanishing too soon.
I am the rising sun,
Infusing life with vibrant hues,
When day has just begun.
I am the shooting star,
Igniting wishes in hearts afar,
No matter who they are.
I am the rustling leaves,
Teaching tales of change and growth,
As the old tree grieves.
I am the constant river,
Flows without fail,
With love to deliver.
I am the towering mountain,
Steadfast and strong,

Fountain of wisdom to attain.
I am the blazing fire,
Igniting passion, burning despair,
Provoking the innermost desire.
I am the peaceful rain,
Washing away the worldly stain,
Nourishing life again.
I am all these various faces,
In essence, the universal spirit,
Rejoicing in divine graces.
I am love,
I am peace,
I am truth,
and joyous release,
The dance of life that never cease.

# *I Am All There Is*

In the deep abyss of infinite mystery,
Beyond the confines of comprehension,
A beacon in the heart of divine unity,
A spark of conscious transcendence.
In the limitless ocean of cosmic sea,
Through the realms of silent reverie,
Unseen, unheard, yet eternally,
I am All,
All that ever can be.
The dance of stars, the galaxy's whirl,
Planets and moons in cosmic swirl,
Silence within, in chaos unfurled,
I am All,
I am the world.
I am the wind that whispers through trees,
The thundering voice in storm's decree,
In the serene silence, the buzzing of bees,
In all that's alive, it is I you see.
I am the flame of love's burning desire,
The spark within that never tires.
The life's essence, its primal fire,
The wellspring of hope, never to expire.
Through joys and sorrows, ebb and flow,

The stream of life, in its endless tow,
From the bloom of youth to aged snow,
In the rhythm of time,
I silently glow.
Unseen I exist, yet known in hearts,
From one we begin, in many we part,
Boundless and free, devoid of charts,
The Divine essence, the ultimate art.
In love and loss, in grief and mirth,
From death to birth, from birth to earth,
From finite forms to boundless worth,
In each heartbeat,
I find rebirth.
Neither separate, nor apart
I remain,
Not confined by space, nor chained by
time's reign,
Unbound by birth, free of death's pain,
I am All,
All there is, again and again.
In you, in me, in each living thing,
In every note that the cosmos sings,
In silent whispers and thunderous roars,
I am All,
All there is, forever more.

# *We Are One*

We walk upon the Earth, different yet the
same,
In heart, in spirit, under the
Divine's endless game.
From mountain peaks to deep oceanic
plains,
Universe echoes the sacred refrain
- We Are One.
Separation is a falsehood, a human decree,
For the sun, the moon, and the air that we
breathe,
See no lines drawn upon the sand,
But celebrate unity throughout this vast
land.
We, the myriad hues of humankind,
From various cultures and faiths are
entwined.
Seeds sown from the Divine garden grand,
Growing together on this shared homeland.
Underneath the veil of our bodies we find,
That it is one single
Soul that defines mankind,
Stretching out to every corner, every sea,

Revealing our shared identity
- We Are One.
Look deep into the eyes of a fellow being,
Beyond physical layers, a unity foreseeing,
Tales of joys, tears, loss and love won,
Reflects our shared journey under the sun.
The waters in the oceans, the leaves on the trees,
The sparkle in stars, the humming of the bees,
Are all whispered stories of creation's song,
Proclaiming the truth we've known all along.
Let's shed our illusions, tear the veil,
Awaken the truth, let love prevail.
Let's weave the world in a loving spun,
Boundless, timeless, knowing
- We Are One.
Each moment, each day, let's stand and be,
A reflection of peace, unity, and harmony.
One humanity under the sun's embrace,
Living the profound truth, in each other's grace.
May we be aware, in the still of our silence,
Echoing unity, the pulse of existence,
For we are not islands, separated, undone,

In the tapestry of life, together we are woven
- We Are One.

# *Together*

In the quiet solitude, the divine chorus echoes,
Together, we glide, souls intertwined with the cosmos.
Dressed in silken threads of celestial twine,
Basking in the ethereal glow of the divine.
Across a constellation canvas, our spirits glide,
Infinite love for one another, no universe can hide.
Togetherness, a celestial melody composed by stardust,
We traverse the ethereal plane, our journey robust.
Our spirits aligned, soaring over cosmic seams,
Embroidered by the Creator in a tapestry of dreams.
We sip the nectar of galaxies far and near,
A divine duet sung, only celestial ears can hear.
Stars cradle our whispers, the cosmos our infinite choir,

Together, we forge the heavenly path, never to tire.
Echoing in our hearts, an eternal verse,
Guided by the Universe, across its expansive diverse.
In our shared ether, our souls illuminate,
A celestial dance, beautifully articulate.
Together we weave through astral hues,
An eternal bond, no cosmic force can lose.
Across dimensions unseen, the connection so pure,
Together in spiritual unity, forever we endure.
For as stars adorn the cosmic dome,
Even when apart, together we'll always be home.

## *Together United*

In the vast ocean of God's great kingdom,
We all, brothers and sisters, each a divine
emblem.
An integral part of this grand orchestra of
life,
Striving through joys and sorrow, triumph
and strife.
We are many shades of faith, under one
God,
Traveling on life's journey, along the same
sod.
Interwoven by threads of love, united in
purpose,
We light up the world, like a celestial cirrus.
Some kneel in prayer, some bow, some
chant,
While others sit still, in tranquil enchant.
Yet we're drawn together, by divine
invitation,
Our hearts echoing with the same jubilation.
Gathering strength from shared
compassion,
Daring to love, in an unmeasured fashion.

In empathy we blossom, with patience we thrive,
Finding God in each soul, as love comes alive.
Though paths may diverge, as destinies unwind,
In the cathedral of heart, a common prayer we find.
Every voice, every whisper, echoes in unity,
Each soul, each heart, yearns for peace in humanity.
We're strands of light, entwined through ages,
United by love, in a story that never ages.
So let us honor each path, each diverse narration,
In our shared quest, for divine elation.
Remember, we're many bodies, but one in Spirit,
God's love binding us all, let's all feel it.
Hand in hand, we stand, across time and space,
Together united, in the wide divine embrace.

## *I See Your Light*

In the quiet depths of the night,
Beneath the silver kiss of moonlight,
I see your light, shining bright,
Guiding me with divine sight.
Stars scattered like sacred seeds,
Celestial echoes of noble deeds,
In their glow, my soul feeds,
You are the light my spirit needs.
In your gaze, infinite grace,
Beyond this human time and space,
Glimmers of the divine I trace,
In the silent serenity of your face.
Waves of love in my heart surge,
As the earthly and heavenly merge,
My soul, to your divine light, it does urge,
Seeking peace, in that celestial purge.
With each beat, your light within grows,
In my soul, a holy river flows,
A journey only the heart knows,
To where the eternal light glows.
With the dawn,
I see your radiance bloom,
Vanquishing darkness, dispelling gloom,
In your light, I find my room,

A beacon in my life's gloom.
Oh, source of all, hear my plight,
Fill me with your radiant light,
Lead me from night into bright,
In your divine love, I find my might.
In silence, I feel your comforting embrace,
In prayer, I find your divine grace,
I see your light in every face,
I am home, in your infinite space.

# Full Moon

Underneath the glistening canvas of stars,
There hung the glorious moon so large,
Whispers of nocturnal secrets and deep
scars,
A nocturnal symphony where darkness was
in charge.
But within that vast realm of dark, there lay,
A sentinel luminous and celestial.
A heavenly lantern amidst the nebula's
ballet,
An astronomical miracle quite terrestrial.
The full moon in its alluring charm,
An orb casting a spectral silvery spell,
Craters etched with a soothing balm,
And upon the quiet earth, a tranquil spell
fell.
Shining amidst the grandeur of cosmic dark,
Reflecting sunlight like an ethereal park,
Emitting whispers of old tales told,
Resurrecting stories of earth's youth bold.
Mankind looks upon it with reverence,
Drawn to the brilliance of its mysterious
trance.

Some finding solace in its stoic might,
Some narrating fables of its crystal light.
As spiritual souls seek solace beneath its
radiant dome,
A humble reminder that this earth is our
home,
Bound by forces, tides and gravities sway,
Unspoken serenity found in its gentle way.
In the sacred silence of this cosmic delight,
Prayers ascend towards its eternal light.
Tales of werewolves, witches and more,
Echo softly in the full moon lore.
Shrouded in mysteries, cloaked with
mystique,
Full moon dances in an enchanting
boutique.
Cradling dreams and shadowed songs,
Bringing a tranquility that rightfully belongs.
Gazing upon its pale sapphire face,
Laying bare, in our universe's embrace.
Unraveling cosmic tapestry's spun,
One with the cosmos, under the
Full Moon's run.
Each crater whispering tales of the
unknown,

Mirroring life's beauty majestically shown.
Like the full moon in our hearts within,
Illuminating the darkness, our own soul's
hymn.

# The Faith Inside

Beneath the mortal veneer, deep within the
cavern of my soul,
Resides a flame, divine and bold, fueling the
faith that keeps me whole.
Like the sun illuminates the day, casting out
the eerie night,
The faith inside clears the haze, giving sight
to blind insight.
When burdens bear down heavy, when
sorrow saps the strength,
When worries weigh like granite stones,
stretching despair to great length.
A tender whisper speaks inside, softly,
soothingly it tells,
In silence lie the answers, where a supreme
spirit dwells.
The winds of worldly trials seek to
extinguish this inner light,
Thrusting waves of cynicism, blurring the
wrong from right.
Yet the flame it dances steadily, for the
tempest it does not fear,

An enduring beacon in life's storm, the faith
inside remains clear.
In this shrine of inner peace, divine love
continues to flow,
Invisible yet perceptible, like a ceaseless
underglow.
Humbled before this mystic force, a moment
of eternity we capture,
Clinging to this radiant faith, basking in its
nurturing rapture.
Beneath the fleshy cloak, hidden in the
chambers of the heart,
Flourishes an everlasting faith, linking the
end back to the start.
So, in our search for meaning, amid the
clamor and the din,
Let's silence our external cries, and seek
the faith within.
In joy and sorrow, in laughter and in tears,
Through the twists and turns of years,
Let this be our guide, our respite, our friend,
This faith inside, on which all can depend.

## *Journey Within*

Within my heart, a silent call
Awakening realms unknown to all.
Beyond the boundaries of flesh and bone,
On an inward journey, all alone.
Journey within, in a world surreal,
Purity and truth its only appeal.
Where wisdom resides, in tranquility
profound,
Beneath layers of silence, whispers are
found.
Like a gentle river that inward flows,
Touching the core, where the eternal glows.
Light within light, an infinite ocean,
A boundless voyage of pure devotion.
Whispers of a silent symphony,
Echoes of an inner mystery.
Every heartbeat a song of love divine,
This sacred journey is yours and mine.
The path of love winds deep and long,
Yet love's sweet voice is the traveler's song.
This pilgrimage within, is a quiet quest,
To seek the true self, the divine guest.
Across the desert of forgetfulness,

Rise mountains of serene blessedness.
A sacred garden, a divine space,
Beyond the self, in a realm of grace.
Traveling beyond thoughts that bind,
Journey within, the soul to find.
To know the self, and the divine align,
This inner voyage, to your soul design.
Love's compass guides, the only light,
Through the darkest depths, into infinite
night.
To the center of self, where love does dwell,
This inner journey, the heart can tell.
For within the heart's deepest recess,
Resides a pure consciousness,
selflessness.
An inward journey, to seek, to explore,
This sacred pilgrimage, forevermore.

## *Let it Go*

In this realm of worldly echoes,
Where human hearts silently weep,
There's a truth deep within us,
A sacred secret we ought to keep.
Do not clutch at your sufferings,
Nor let resentments fester and grow,
Embrace the divine lesson,
Breathe deep and let it go.
For no darkness is permanent,
Every storm brings a clearing sky.
In the dance of cosmic forces,
Each sorrow is followed by a sigh.
Know this: You are not your losses,
Not the wounds nor the shadowy fear,
You are light manifesting,
Through the human form, so dear.
Do not allow yourself to falter,
Underneath the burden you bear.
Gaze instead at the infinite cosmos,
At the boundless love laid bare.
Understand that forgiveness,
Is a divine power bestowed,
Upon the hearts of the gentle,

Where kindness freely flowed.
Be not tethered to anguish,
Lift your eyes and let it show,
In this universe so vast and tender,
Find courage and let it go.
Like the blossoms in the wild wind,
Releasing their seeds to the unknown,
Trust in the flow of existence,
Let go and let God's grace be shown.
For you are more than earthly torment,
A spiritual being learning to grow,
Hold faith in the dance of existence,
Just breathe, surrender, and let it go.
Dwell not in the chambers of yesterday,
Where old wounds silently echo.
Welcome the dawn of divine love,
Inhale, exhale, and let it go.
For the greatest act of courage,
Is not to win, but to forego,
In the spiritual symphony of life,
Sing loud your heart's song, and let it go.

## *Touch The Sky*

On the quest to touch the sky,
Our soul embarks on a journey so high,
Bare feet to the earth, head aimed towards
the light,
Engaging in a silent and divine flight.
Each morning is the canvas of an unseen
art,
Each breath, a song that starts in the heart,
Residing not in mortal limits, nor dreads,
We are more than mere beings, holding our
heads.
Underneath our palms is the warmth of
humanity,
Etched on our souls, is the map of eternity,
And, deep within, radiates a golden light,
It is there, in our true selves, free and bright.
Reaching the corners of the heart's tranquil
shrine,
As serene as the sea, pure as divine,
Vulnerable in faith, strong in submission,
Shimmering in the silver aura of our
intuition.
Veins pulsing with the cosmos rhythm,

A galaxy exists within, we are but its emblem,
Connected by cords of the love light, so intense,
Vibrating with the echo of universal resonance.
In silence, in stillness, in the hymns we utter,
Lies an immortal flame that does not flicker,
In this endless expanse of a single moment,
Dance, O souls! In joy, in astonishment.
Remember, we are not this body, not this guise,
But luminous entities, born of starlit skies,
One with the sun, moon, and the swirling cosmos,
Surrendering to the Divine, in Her we repose.
We reach to touch the sky, ever so gently,
In our quest for oneness, exploring divinity,
In silence we discover, in love we unite,
Dancing with the stars, in the moon's soft light.
With grace in our hearts, a prayer on our lips,

We continue the journey of countless trips,
Ever onward, beyond realms and spheres,
In pursuit of the Infinite, far beyond mortal years.

# Diamonds in The Sky

From the velvety darkness they shine,
These diamonds suspended in the divine.
Glimmers of hope in the tranquil night,
Reflecting God's glory with pure delight.
Celestial gems sparkling afar,
Tales of life written in every star.
The heavens open their storybook,
A visual symphony if we dare look.
There, God paints dreams with cosmic
brush,
Silencing the world into a hush.
There, through stardust and dark we see,
A magnificent tapestry woven lovingly.
Those diamond-studded arms that stretch
wide,
In which mysteries and truths reside.
From birth of stars to their solemn end,
Galactic poems, they faithfully send.
Each twinkling jewel, a solitaire,
A testament of Its Infinite care.
With every light year, with every day,
God whispers love in Its subtle way.
Diamonds in the sky, yet hearts aflame,

Shimmering echoes of Its holy name.
Meditate on these constellations bright,
Feel the presence in the silent night.
Though silent, they voice cosmic hymns,
A soothing balm for all earthly whims.
This divine display of celestial art,
Is God's love letter to the human heart.
Thus, they're not mere stones ablaze,
But, God's language is in stellar phase.
The diamonds in the sky are high,
As messengers of the Most High.
As we gaze up to the stars above,
May we receive Its radiant love.
For diamonds in the sky aren't merely pretty,
They're verses from the Universe's divine ditty.

## *Sapphire Night*

Under the star-spangled shroud of sapphire
night,
Among a garden jeweled with silver light,
Awakens in me, a tune of the divine,
I roam in pursuit of love, subtle and benign.
Silent whispers in the rhythm of the wind,
Subtle gestures in the flutter of leaves
pinned,
Speaking volumes to my wandering heart,
Secrets of the universe, waiting to impart.
Echoing the lullaby of cosmic tide,
Chanting verses of unity far and wide,
My spirit flies towards the heavens
unbarred,
Lost and found in an infinity starred.
Every pulsating constellation far and deep,
Every celestial saga the comets keep,
Every quivering wavelength of milky hue,
Dances a ballet of creation, ever new.
Star-kissed paths illuminate the maze,
That binds our destiny in enigmatic haze.
Pulsing hearts beat to a symphony
unknown,
Orchestrated by the divine, tenderly shown.

And in this cathedral of eternal twilight,
Bathing in the glory of radiant moonlight,
My spirit unearths treasures of the mystic
night,
Drinking wisdom from the chalice of celestial
sight.
Through sapphire spheres and the velvet
dome,
In cosmic waters, I discover my home.
Cloaked in divine raiment of tranquility,
Bathing in wisdom, imbued with serenity.
An ardent voyage across the astral sea,
An infinite dance with the divinity,
This sapphire night, more than just a starry
veil,
Is the womb of wisdom, where dreams
prevail.
Drenched in the sonnet of ethereal light,
I find my faith in the sapphire night,
Beyond the realm of fleeting worldly sight,
Resides an endless love, eternal and bright.

# My Wish

Oh Divine essence of the cosmic lore,
Of galaxies unseen and oceans yet to
explore,
Guide my humble self as I navigate life,
And with your infinite wisdom, soften strife.
I ask not for silver or bountiful gold,
Nor fame and riches to behold,
My heart seeks rather for truths divine,
The subtle secrets of thine own design.
Grant me vision to perceive your sign,
Within all existence, a harmony divine,
A clarity to grasp the dawn's soft hue,
A sight that penetrates the illusion's untrue.
Give me strength when my hope is low,
For in the darkest hours, true faith grow.
Bestow upon me a resilient will,
To learn from trials, never to shrivel.
Guide me on a path of charity,
For a compassionate heart radiates clarity.
A seed of kindness when nurtured and
sown,
Unfolds a garden of virtues, beautifully
grown.

Above all else, O Universal light,
Clothe me in humility, purge pride from my
sight.
To walk among men in modest attire,
Free from arrogance, empty of self-desire.
May I comprehend the boundless, be still,
In silent wonder at thy divine will,
Not simply to exist, but to understand,
The beauty of living according to your grand
plan.
Such is my wish, O Maker of All,
Upon your mercy, I earnestly call,
Guide my steps in this world immense,
To fulfill your decree with humility and
grace.

# *I Wish For All*

In the grand cosmic dance, under twinkling
stars so bright,
I weave my desires and wishes into the
velvet night.
Here, standing at the precipice of universal
space,
I raise my hands to the heavens, to an
infinite grace.
I wish for all to discover, their spiritual spark,
The divine inner truth, that guides us in the
dark.
I yearn for hearts to awaken, their endless
potential,
With kindness and love, sincere and
essential.
I dream of a world, filled with peace and
serenity,
Where every soul finds solace in shared
eternity.
I wish for strength and wisdom, for each
soul on earth,
So they may find true fulfillment and infinite
worth.

I desire unity, compassion to unfold,
Where acceptance is cherished, more
precious than gold.
May all recognize their value, in this vast
cosmic play,
Where each is an actor, in an ageless ballet.
I yearn for tolerance, empathy to prevail,
As we traverse life's journey, together we
sail.
May joy and contentment echo in each soul,
Mending hearts, building bridges, making
spirits whole.
I pray for love to permeate, each atom, each
cell,
So all would know its power, its sacred,
gentle swell.
May forgiveness replace grudges, let no
hate reside,
In this divine communion, where love and
peace collide.
I wish for all, that darkness shall dissipate,
Under the celestial light of faith and fate.
As I surrender my desires into the cosmic
vast,

I am humbled by the present, enlightened
by the past.
Oh, may my wish reach the highest of highs,
Upwards it travels, into the eternal skies.
The stars will carry it, beyond the realm of
space,
I wish for all, God's infinite grace.

## *You're Unstoppable*

In the deep well of silence, divine truth lays
awake,
Waiting for the dawn, the shackles to break,
Believe in the divine, my dear friend, for thy
sake,
For it whispers to thee, you're unstoppable,
no mistake.
Radiating rays of sun, mirrored in your eyes,
Each and every morning, the grand sun
shall rise,
Every setback, every fall, each good or bad,
Like the undying phoenix, you're born from
the ashes,
don't be sad.
Beneath the dust of aching sorrow, pure
love uncurls,
A spectrum of brilliant hues, more precious
than pearls,
Allow thyself to trust, to give, to take,
With undaunted courage, it's your destiny to
make.
Embrace each tear, each wound, each war,
Every hidden struggle, each scar,

Deep within the rubble, there lies a shining
star,
An indomitable spirit, that's what you truly
are.
Tangled up in sorrow, or floating in the sky,
Remember your inner compass, that cannot
lie,
Though the tide may turn, the sun may fall,
Like the unfailing ocean, you're greater than
it all.
Girded by divine hands, lit with a sacred
light,
There is an unseen strength that makes thy
spirit bright.
Lean onto thy soul, within it dwells the sage,
An ethereal force, the Universe's open
page.
Thou art an atom in the universe,
the universe within an atom too,
An enigma that remains, each morning born
anew,
Seek not what's not you, don't let your faith
be robbed,
Believe in yourself, and in your divine light,
for you're  unstoppable, blessed by God.

# *You're Unstoppable Joy*

Awaken, child of the cosmos, on the crest of
a golden dawn,
Be cradled by the gentle hum of eternity,
from the night until the morn.
Remember your worth, that surpasses gold
and gem,
You are of divine origin, in the cosmos is
your stem.
Dance in the gentle wind, like a flame that
cannot be put out,
Revel in your strength, remove all lingering
doubt.
Through love and loss, in sunshine and in
rain,
Your spirit's fire blazes on, untamed and
without restrain.
Step boldly forward in life's grand ballet,
Your existence sings a song of joy that can't
be cast away.
Every pulse of your heart is a testament to
love,

A symphony of splendor, blessed by the cosmos above.

You are love embodied, clothed in stardust and grace,

Reflections of the cosmos are etched upon your face.

Though trials may come, like waves upon the sea,

Your unstoppable joy makes every burden flee.

For within you lies an energy, resolute and strong,

An echoing, silent anthem that's been yours all along.

Sing forth this melody, pure and sublime,

You're a beacon of unstoppable joy, transcending space and time.

When the sun dips low, and shadows claim the light,

Yours is the joy that blazes, a lantern in the night.

Dwell not in the valley of fear, doubt or decay,

Embrace your inner radiance, let it light your way.

In moments of sorrow, or the highest ecstasy,
Yours is the joy unquenchable, boundless as the sea.
Roaring like a tempest, soft as a lullaby's tune,
Your joy, it burns brighter than a thousand afternoons.
So let your spirit dance upon the earth's wide stage,
Remember you're an endless joy, immune to rust or age.
Forever in your essence, flows a joy untold,
You're unstoppable, enduring, as ancient as days of old.
A beacon to the cosmos, to stars both near and far,
Illuminated by the radiant light, of the divinity you are.
Clothed in resplendent stardust, of wisdom and delight,
You're an eternal, unstoppable joy, a star burning bright.

# *The Songs of Love*

In the sacred cathedral of the heart,
Resounds a hymn, divine and soft.
In the highest echelon of the soul's art,
Sings the songs of love aloft.
Beneath the firmament of dreams
unspoken,
Beneath the tranquil celestial night,
Whispered are words of love, the golden
token,
Of a divine connection, bathed in divine
light.
By the rosy dawn's ethereal glow,
In silence and whispers that grace the morn,
With affection that the angels know,
A song of love, in our hearts is born.
Often, we walk in realms of sorrow,
Lost in a labyrinth of doubts so grave.
Yet the songs of love sing of tomorrow,
Where exists an everlasting love so brave.
Through the tunnel of despair, shines a
light,
Gentle whispers that in our souls dwell.
In this realm of eternal twilight,

The songs of love, of hope, they tell.
Not confined by the terrestrial plane,
Beyond the grasp of worldly sight,
Through sorrow, joy, through loss and gain,
The songs of love persist in flight.
Transcending the barriers of the corporeal,
Breaching the dimensions of the seen and
unseen,
In our hearts, an anthem immortal,
Sings the song of love, so serene.
In every soul, a symphony resounds,
Of tenderness that time will not efface.
The melody of love that knows no bounds,
In the soul, eternally takes place.
For love is the melody, the sacred verse,
A symphony of celestial harmonies blend,
With each beat of the heart, it does
rehearse,
The songs of love that never end.

# The Song of Goddess

In the canvas of cosmic night,
There weaves a celestial light.
She sings in silence, radiant and bright,
A song of harmony in the perpetual flight.
Beyond the mortal frame,
Existence echoes her sacred name.
An echo vibrating from a hidden flame,
Goddess, mother, essence, the same.
The universe kneels in silent prayer,
Enchanted by her love so rare.
Unseen she mends each tear,
Her blessings, like breath, in the air.
She's the dream that paints the sky,
The melody of the lark's soft cry.
She is the light in the weary traveler's eye,
The sunset's grace, the dawn's shy sigh.
She resides in the echo of our heartbeat,
In the soul where silence and music meet.
The secret source of all things sweet,
Where divine and earthly subtly greet.
She paints in colors bold and fair,
In hues of love, on the canvas bare.
With tender touch and soothing care,

She strokes the world with an artist's flare.
Each song she sings, a spell to weave,
With whispers in the morning's heave.
A gentle voice that prompts to believe,
In magic, mystery, love's reprieve.
Goddess divine, hear my plea,
Let my soul in your melody be free.
Grant me eyes that truly see,
Your radiant song, the key to Thee.
Hear my prayers in this sacred night,
Let your wisdom be my guiding light.
Embrace me in your love's divine might,
My heart echoes the song of your delight.
A silent hymn in the heart of creation,
You're the melody of all adoration.
From atom to star, in every nation,
Sings your song, the cosmic vibration.
Your name in each breeze softly uttered,
Your grace in each bloom brightly fluttered,
Goddess divine, your love has cluttered,
The cosmic orchestra, in harmony,
shuddered.
We bow to thee in deepest reverence,
O cosmic mother, your love is our
sustenance.

To thy melody, we find deliverance,
In the song of the Goddess, our purest
essence.

# *Find Yourself*

In the realm of the rising sun,
Beyond the realm of mortal man,
Seek you a path not treaded upon,
Unfurl the sails of your soul's caravan.
In the chamber of your inner being,
Awake from your slumber, divine and wise,
Look not outside, cease your fleeing,
The truth you seek, in your heart it lies.
Embark on a journey of profound serenity,
Amidst chaos, seek tranquility,
Shed the shackles of falsity and vanity,
Seek yourself in splendid singularity.
In silence, surrender to your soul's song,
Seek not in the crowd where you belong,
Within you are boundless and strong,
All answers within, for nothing you've done
wrong.
The embers of divinity brightly glow,
Beneath the layers of your human woe,
Fan it gently, let it grow,
Find yourself, in its luminous show.
Bathe in the sacred river of self-knowledge,
Embark on this never-ending pilgrimage,

Honor your soul's ancient lineage,
Write your destiny on life's empty page.
Seek within the kingdom of your heart,
Where God's whisper is your guide and
chart,
Within your soul's crypt, pry apart,
Discover your divine work of art.
Surrender to your soul's soft sound,
With courage let your spirit unbound,
Only then can truth be found,
Find yourself on this holy ground.
In the realm of the silent star,
A traveler you are, come from far,
Finding yourself is not a war,
It's embracing who you truly are.

## *New Beginnings*

A new day unfolds with a subtle yawn,
Bathing the world in a dew-laced dawn,
Beginnings anew with the light of grace,
In this ever-turning cosmic space.
Each morning holds a holy hymn,
As the darkness to brightness brim,
In silent whispers of gratitude,
We bow to life's magnitude.
Sprouting seed and breaking shell,
On fertile soils of hope, we dwell,
Summoned by the universe's hymn,
We rise, in divinity, we swim.
Life, a divine script well-wrought,
Of lessons learned and wisdom taught,
Each breath, a moment divinely spun,
Each heartbeat, a victory won.
We gaze at the sun with reverent awe,
Feel the earth beneath with loving claw,
This spinning sphere, this boundless
expanse,
Invites us all in a celestial dance.
Glistening rivers and mountains high,
Reflect the spirit's longing sigh,

Blossoming blooms, star-spangled skies,
Echoes the divine in tranquil guise.
As we step forward, free from sin,
There is a holiness that begins,
Touched by the purity of Its gaze,
A newborn soul in eternal days.
Cherishing the gentle surrender,
To a journey, soft and tender,
Dawn and dusk, dark and light,
Every beginning is an invite to the fight.
A call to bravery, faith, and love,
Guided by powers from above,
For every beginning, blessed or strained,
In God's wisdom, is ordained.
Each day's a testament of Its art,
Carved in the canvas of the heart,
In beginnings new, the Divine resides,
In Its embrace, our spirit confides.
For every dawn holds a promise anew,
To discover, to seek, to find what's true,
In new beginnings, the spirit is reborn,
With the first light of every dawn.

# *It's My Time*

Awakened by the radiant sun, amidst
celestial chime,
Into a world of joy and love, it's my soul's
sublime time.
The angels, in hushed whispers, affirm my
divine worth,
Time to spread my glistening wings, rise
high from this Earth.
Beyond the trivial boundaries, where mere
bodies define,
I find myself resplendent, where spirit and
God intertwine.
No shackles of judgment can hold me, nor
ties of false shame,
It's my time to blaze and shimmer, a divinely
sparked flame.
Within my heart resides the cosmos, the
nebula of love,
Guiding light from stars above, gracing me
from the heavens above.
I resonate with the ethereal melody, of
existence's sublime rhyme,

Flooded with the divine truth, it's my time, it's my prime.
Past, present, and future merge in this singular beat,
It's my time to realize I'm whole, perfectly complete.
My soul's in eternal dance with life, each rhythm so divine,
Unveiling the veil of illusion, realizing the divine design.
I hold no fear for my journey, let the shadows sway,
In the glow of inner light, darkness dissolves away.
The divinity within me glimmers, whispers of the Divine,
Carved from sacred light, yes, it's indeed my time.
May this spirit-infused melody reach all who have the ears,
Embrace the call of the Divine, dismiss your primal fears.
Today, tomorrow, and every moment, my soul shines with celestial prime,

Indeed, yes indeed, now and forever, it's my very own divine time.

# *I Will Shine*

In the dark recesses of life's dense forest,
There's a whisper of light that hovers
modest,
Amongst the shadows and hollow silence,
I feel my spirit bloom in resilience.
Stumbling on jagged paths of despair,
I sought solace but found only vacant
stares,
Lost in the wilderness, amidst fears
untamed,
A faint spark ignited, a spirit untamed.
No longer, it uttered, will I retreat,
To the crumbling corners of defeat,
I am born of stardust, woven in light,
Embedded with resilience, strong in might.
I am not the desolation of a star that fell,
But a beacon of light, enduring, swell.
Though struggles may quell and hope
seems dire,
Inside me is an inextinguishable fire.
Each knock of challenge, every tribulation,
Is but a forge for my soul's formation,
In sorrow's ashes and agony's brine,

Like a Phoenix, I will rise, I will shine.
For I am the child of cosmic skies,
Cradled by sunsets, soothed by sunrise.
I am born of love, compassion my rhyme,
I am not just survival, but the essence of
time.
Through life's tempest, may it roar or
whisper,
I shall radiate, glow, shimmer, glister,
For darkness can only inhabit the space,
Until I replace it, with my luminous grace.
In my journey, though I am confined,
By the thorny past and fear unrefined,
Within this vessel, raw and divine,
Forever, oh forever, I will shine.

# *Open Up*

In the silent hush of a tranquil morn,
Open up to the blessings that the day has
sworn.
Allow your spirit to taste the feast,
Of the soft sunlight in the east.
Open up to the voice divine,
Which speaks in whispers through the vine.
Let it echo in your sacred hall,
Rising and falling with the daylight's call.
Open up to the eternal love,
Streaming ceaselessly from the heavens
above.
Let its light pervade your weary soul,
And your fragmented self, it shall console.
Open up to the universe grand, In all its
marvel, take a stand.
Bathe in the celestial energy's tide,
And let its wisdom be your guide.
Open up to the serenity within,
Free yourself from life's din.
Discover the treasure you carry inside,
In that quiet place, let your spirit abide.
Open up to the symphony of the spheres,

Harmonizing beautifully for unseen ears.
Resonate with their frequency high,
Transcend into a dance with the sky.
Open up to the teachings of the breeze,
Of surrender, patience, and a soul at ease.
Sailing smoothly with life's current,
Emerging stronger, wise and fervent.
Open up to the cycle of seasons,
To change, decay, and life's reasons.
To grow and flourish, to fade and fall,
The cyclical dance, experienced by all.
Open up to your radiant essence,
The divine light that breaks all pretense.
Radiate that love so vast and deep,
Touch the stars, awaken from sleep.
So open up, let your spirit be free,
Gaze upon the beauty of the cosmic sea.
Let the whispers of the divine resound,
In the silent chapel of your heart, let it
abound.

# *Open Mind*

In the realms where mysteries unfold,
Through silence, whispers are told.
Of realms unseen and stories untold,
By the curious, by the brave, by the open
mind.
No earthly wisdom, no crowns of gold,
Can fathom truth's priceless hold.
Through layers of the world, so old,
Lies the essence, by the open mind behold.
Open minds like blossoms unfold,
Embracing knowledge, secrets untold.
Shedding the bias, let prejudices be old,
Exploring truth in the diversity we hold.
The mystical energy in stars bold,
Spirals of galaxies, celestial unfold.
Within, outside, stories yet untold,
Seen only by an open mind, we are told.
Across spiritual boundaries, ever bold,
Flows the stream of consciousness, ancient
and old.
Harmony in differences, love uncontrolled,
Realized in depth by an open mind's hold.
Feel the oneness, as mystics foretold,

In every creature, in the young and the old.
Love, kindness, virtues more valuable than gold,
Experienced purely through an open mind bold.
Sculpted by life, by tales, manifold,
Guided by starlight, in twilight's threshold.
Where dreams blend into realities, remold,
Is where you'll find, the awakening of an open mind.
Open your mind, let spirit take hold,
For truth and love can't be bought or sold.
Like a divine map that slowly unfolds,
Showing paths of enlightenment, to open minds, bold.
In the chambers of the heart, the sacred abode,
Underneath the façade that worldly robes.
Thrive secrets of the cosmos, subtly stowed,
Unraveled quietly by the seekers with an open mind.
Let the curtains rise, let the illusion erode,
It's in our shared stories, true riches are bestowed.

A harmonious orchestra of existence we decode,
With each note struck, resonates an open mind.

## *Creating New Doors*

In a realm beyond mere mortal view,
Exists a landscape ever fresh, ever new,
Where truth dances freely under love's sun,
And harmony's song is beautifully sung.
Oh, seek, oh seeker of the radiant soul,
Where essence shines brighter than earthly
gold.
Beneath the thin veneer of human guise,
Divinity's door lies in disguise.
Life, a labyrinth of illusions and tests,
Urges the heart on a sacred quest.
Yet each challenge, every fear, every loss,
Serves but as keys to the wisdom we cross.
Our joys and sorrows, wounds and graces,
Are reflections of our deeper spaces.
In the quiet stillness of your heart's core,
Lie the keys to unlock the spiritual door.
Once unlocked, there you'll find the flame,
A light that flickers yet stays the same.
From each heartbeat, a rhythmic song,
Chanting, you were divine all along.
With each loving action, we create,
A door to a realm where love resonates.

Our purpose then, simple, yet grand,
To birth love's kingdom on earthly land.
And so we journey, from morning till night,
Crafting doors in love's holy light.
No door too small, no effort unseen,
In the eyes of the divine, forever serene.
From each hardship and every delight,
Blossoms a portal of resplendent light.
We are the artisans of our fate,
Carving new doors in the walls of hate.
Open, then, your heart wide and clear,
Every pulse beckoning divinity near.
Embrace the trials, for in every score,
Lies the chance to create a new door.
Love unending, boundless, ever true,
In this celestial dance, forever continues,
Crafting with care in the cosmos vast,
New doors to a future unsurpassed.
In the ethereal garden of humanity's quest,
Let's craft new doors with loving zest,
So each soul might one day find,
A path to peace within their own mind.
As we sow these seeds of divine lore,
Our legacy remains evermore.
Not in worldly riches, not in power,

But in the creation of love's sacred door.

# *Creating New Pathways*

As I journey through the land of the Divine,
Casting my footprints in sacred sands of
time,
Seeking a space where peace and love
align,
Carving new pathways, sublimely divine.
Guided by faith, and hope as my map,
Engraving footsteps where angels once sat.
Climbing the mountains, basking in the
glow,
Creating new pathways, as the gentle rivers
flow.
Stars as my lantern, moon as my guide,
Journeying through cosmos, taking all in
stride.
Whispers of wisdom, echoes of ancient
tales,
Marking my path, where truth unveils.
Carving new pathways, beyond what eyes
can see,
A trail that is filled with grace and harmony.
Through the mystical valley and the
sapphire sea,

I walk with purpose, becoming who I wish to
be.
I explore, I grow, in this infinite realm,
Holding God's wisdom like a ship's sturdy
helm.
Through silence and stillness, life's ultimate
goal,
Creating new pathways, in the landscape of
the soul.
And in this celestial dance, where souls
intertwine,
Emerges the essence, truly divine.
Though pathways may shift, as
constellations rearrange,
The quest for inner truth, shall never
change.
So, with each step, the soul shall strive,
Creating new pathways, keeping faith alive.
As God as my witness, love as my guide,
I tread on new pathways, with the universe
by my side.

## *This is Your Song*

Beneath the mantle of azure skies,
Unfurls the grand symphony of the sunrise,
An enchanting dance of heavenly hue,
Crafted by The Divine just for you.
This is your song, the melody of life,
Hummed through days of joy and strife.
Echoing in valleys, in canyons deep,
Caressing the soul, coaxing dreams from
sleep.
In gentle whispers of the waning moon,
In playful rustling of leaves in the afternoon,
Through roaring thunder and quietest rain,
Your song rings out, unchained by pain.
Breathe it in, let the notes flow,
Become the harmony, let the rhythm grow.
This celestial score, this heavenly hymn,
An ethereal serenade, echoes from within.
Your song, your journey, an ever-moving
sea,
Holds the echo of laughter, a prayer on
bended knee.
Sculpted by The Creator's artist's hand,
Singing the essence of a soul so grand.

Look not outside, seek not in vain,
Your song resonates in the heart's sacred
domain.
Gentle, strong, filled with grace,
An expression of love in this cosmic space.
Dance to your song, celebrate the morn,
For every new day, a soul is reborn.
Find the music, create the symphony,
Your life, your song, a beautiful epiphany.
Oh mortal being, fear not the long night,
For your song endures, a beacon of pure
light.
Gifted from the Heavens, it's forever your
call,
Your spirit's echo in this Universe's grand
hall.
Rejoice in the chorus, give voice to your
truth,
This is your song, an eternal song of youth.
Play on, seraphic spirit, from morning until
dusk,
This is your song, an ode of heavenly trust.

# *Believe*

In realms unseen, where dreams whisper true,
Across the star-studded vault of cobalt blue,
A faith unseen but ever present,
With the potency of an ethereal crescent.
Can you hear it? The call so subtle,
Chiming from celestial temple, so humble.
Believe, oh soul, in miracles unbound,
Where divine whispers echo with profound.
Believe in paths adorned with divine light,
Where angels tread in robes of pure white,
In dreams woven with ethereal thread,
In whispers from the ancients, the celestial spread.
Fear not the mire, the shadow, the shroud,
But embrace the struggle, emerge unbowed.
Look to the stars, to the mystic tide,
Trust in Its promise, be your soul's guide.
The divine architect scripts your fate,
Carved in the cosmos, neither early nor late.
The celestial harp plays your song,
In divine symphony where all belong.

Embrace love, not merely to receive,
But to illuminate, to give, to believe.
And in the mirror of your soul shall reflect,
A cosmic radiance of love and respect.
Oh believer, ever blessed, ever bright,
Bound by faith, shining in Its divine light.
With courage profound and trust deep-
rooted,
Sail on, blessed one, divinely suited.
Trust the journey, embrace the dream,
Drunk on love, bathed in starbeam.
Oh, to believe is to find the unseen,
In the embrace of divine, in the spaces
between.
So, tread softly upon this hallowed earth,
Value love's pricelessness, acknowledge its
worth.
Unseen by eyes, yet felt so keen,
This is faith, this is to believe, forever
serene.

# *Unity*

In the depths of hearts where Love softly
lies,
Bathed in divine essence and Heaven's
sunrise,
Unity unfolds as the essence of life,
Where every soul dances, free from strife.
Unity, dear friends, isn't a theory learned,
But the spark within, ceaselessly yearned,
A sweet surrender to Love's divine plan,
An inner truth woven in the cosmic clan.
Through unity we rise, through unity we
glow,
In unity, the mightiest rivers flow,
Our souls merging in celestial harmony,
A symphony composed by divinity.
One rhythm, one heartbeat, echoing God's
song,
In unity, dear ones, we all belong,
Mirroring the stars, a tapestry so wide,
A boundless cosmos in each soul resides.
Oh, sing with the sun, dance with the moon,
To the rhythm of unity, the universal tune,
Join the constellation of souls ablaze,

Unite in love's eternal praise.
For we are the rivers, the mountains, the sky,
One with all, no boundary can imply,
A part of each sunset's golden hues,
Unity, dear ones, is our muse.
Let us bow to the East, turn towards the West,
With one shared prayer swelling in our chest,
Unity, dear ones, in this journey we strive,
For through unity, Love comes alive.
Remember, we are woven from the same thread,
Linked to each other, in love and spirit fed,
Born from the cosmos, kissed by divine light,
Through unity, we journey into the infinite night.
From atom to stars, in unity we dance,
Unveiled, in the hands of divine romance,
With unity we shine, like a pearl in God's hand,
Love is the law, Unity the command.

## *Peace Within*

In the midst of chaos, clamor and noise,
In the swirl of battles, trials and worldly joys,
Through valleys deep, and mountains steep,
There's a peace within that I constantly
seek.
Amid the clamoring crowd, under the cosmic
shroud,
Though roars the thunder, wild and loud,
Within my heart, there's a whisper soft,
In hushed silence, love aloft.
The world may shout, may rail and scream,
Toss me within its tempestuous dream.
Yet within my soul, an unbroken hymn,
A tender serenity, unwavering, dim.
I find a strength in tranquil prayers,
In soothing winds and subtle airs.
Beneath the moon, 'midst twinkling stars,
Unseen forces heal unseen scars.
Walking in gardens, wild and free,
Through the latticed patterns of every tree,
In mirrored waters, reflecting skies,
Therein true peace always lies.
With every sunrise, with every dawn,
In the golden dusk, in the whispers of fawn,

Within the heart of the fluttering dove,
I am reminded of Its undying love.
Though world upon world may rise and fall,
He who created, controls them all.
And within Its grasp, safe and warm,
My spirit finds calm amidst the storm.
Through earthly toils, through tears and
pain,
There's a quiet solace that I attain,
The peace within, the heart's sweet hymn,
It is God's love, flowing from within.
In faith, in hope, in humble trust,
When earthly ties return to dust,
One thing remains, steadfast and bright,
The eternal love, the eternal light.
Peace within, O cherished treasure,
Bestowed by the Divine, in full measure,
Not just a whisper in the wind,
But the soothing balm, where life begins.
From deep within, let it overflow,
Guiding us where we ought to go.
Our compass in life's churning sea,
Peace within, eternally.

## *Off World Beings*

Among the stars, high and twinkling,
Where light dances in celestial chorus,
Beyond the scope of human understanding,
There, reside the off-world beings of
wonderous.
Unseen by naked eyes, untouched by
mortal skin,
Hidden realms of cosmic beauty they reside
within,
Fleeting, ethereal, just a whisper in the
wind,
Mystic entities, neither enemy nor kin.
They dance to rhythms of quasars, pulsars
and black holes,
Existing in dimensions, surpassing earthly
goals,
Clothed in gowns of nebulae, wearing stellar
crowns,
Interstellar children, in galaxies abound.
Under foreign suns they kneel to pray,
Speak languages, light years away,
Worshipping not deities of golden splendor,

But forces raw and wild, untamed and
tender.
Can we fathom their dreams, painted in
stardust,
Can we echo their songs, of cosmic trust?
Through wormholes and through times'
vortex swirled,
Theirs is the unheard symphony of the
universe, unfurled.
Who knows what prayers they've lifted to
strange moons,
Who understands their laughter, their
otherworldly tunes?
And yet in every vibration of celestial might,
They exude, permeate love and pure light.
From constellations far, yet so close to
heart,
Yet what lies between is not a charted part,
Space is but illusion, and time but a veil,
In the dance of cosmic kinship, love shall
always prevail.
Unreachable, perhaps, to our earthly grasp,
In dreams, we share their ethereal clasp,
Bound not by matter, not by solid form,
In the essence of spirit, we are reborn.

O' you celestial children, shower your love
upon us,
Though you exist beyond our reach, and
beyond our thus,
Speak to our souls in stardust kissed rhyme,
As we, the children of Earth, seek our place
in cosmic time.

## *Wings Guide Me*

In the veil of earthly night,
Under the glowing stars so bright,
With whispers of the gentle wind,
An internal pilgrimage I begin.
Wings guide me, gilded and grand,
Feathered tales of distant lands,
Ascend my spirit to sacred height,
Lead me onward through star-studded night.
Breath of life and divine light,
Into this dark, instill thy sight,
Fill my vessel, end the plight,
In serenity's soothing, healing light.
Golden tapestry of destiny,
Intertwined threads of eternity,
Oh, guardian of celestial creed,
Guide me, in grace and good deed.
Speak not in tongues, but silence profound,
Where understanding in solace is found.
Illuminate this winding path,
Lead me through aftermath.
Show me the vista of sacred dreams,
Cross galaxies and cosmic streams,
Tales of love, redemption true,
Embodied in every celestial hue.

Awaken the purpose within my soul,
Whisper tales that make me whole.
Illuminate my mind's night sky,
Teach me how to soar, not just to fly.
In trials of the dark and challenging tide,
May I walk with faith by my side.
For beneath the cloak of the ethereal divine,
Life's essence whispers, Child, you are mine.
Carry me forth on resplendent wing,
Lend me your strength, and songs to sing.
For in faith and the heart's brave fight,
Lie the stories of love, inscribed in light.
Wings guide me through eternity,
Towards divine love, towards serenity,
Each beat echoes of the love I feel,
In this journey, in this heavenly reel.
As dawn approaches, gently you'll guide,
My soul's voyage, the spiritual divide.
Wings guide me, through celestial tide,
Towards home, to love's eternal reside.

## *Invoke Grace*

Upon this stage of life and light,
As morning lifts her shrouded veil,
May grace invoke divine delight
Where faith is pure, and love prevails.
Oh Spirit grand in heaven's glow,
With harmony and light infused,
Bestow thy blessing and thy flow,
Where aching hearts have been bruised.
Speak peace to weary, fragile souls,
Nourish hearts that fear has repressed.
Renew their vigor, their shattered hopes,
And with your mercy, grant them rest.
Within this realm of existence,
Grant us the strength to navigate,
Illuminate the road of persistence,
Invoking grace at each twist and gate.
In this play of destiny and chance,
We beseech thee, God of Divine Dance,
Show us the steps of your sacred dance,
In the music of celestial romance.
Make the soft echo of our pleas,
Reach beyond the azure skies,

Like sweet fragrance carried by the breeze,
Or a dawn's first song as day complies.
Embrace us in your radiant gaze,
Shower us with compassion's rain.
As your grace we do invoke,
Make whole our spirit, ease our pain.
For grace is not of earned estate,
It's God's love, deep, intimate,
Invoke it with a soul aflame,
In divine Love's sacred name.
A hymn of invocation this, Echoing through
the abyss,
Calling forth the dawn of grace,
To illuminate this sacred place.
Within each beat of heart, invoke,
A wordless prayer, a promise spoke,
Embraced in grace, immersed in light,
Loved and blessed by sacred night.
Through the veil of earthy plight,
Invoke thy grace, and with its light,
May we bloom in Love's great might,
In reverence of Divine delight.

## *Dancing Barefoot*

In the grandeur of midnight, beneath the halo of moonlight,
A spirit dances barefoot, traversing on the ethereal delight.
Murmurs of her silk robe whisper stories of yore,
Her eyes radiate joy, mirroring constellations of the starlit night.
Stars envy her celestial charm, her soothing mystic flame,
An aura gentle and tranquil, her name as rare as the rarest gem.
The silhouette of the whispering willow applauds her humble might,
As she swirls, tumbles, and twirls, she loses herself to the infinite night.
With grace she steps on shards of shattered fears,
Through each dancing moment, she unveils hidden years.
Ethereal wings of hope caress her tender soul,
She is the ballet of divine whispers, making the cosmos whole.

Eloquent is her journey through the
enchanted Milky Way,
Her rhythm as harmonic as the grand
symphony of the day.
Nature breathes her in, worshipping her with
sheer delight,
The euphoria in her soul reflects in the
gentle sea of the starlight.
Every gentle sigh of wind acknowledges her
earthly realm,
The moon whispers secrets into her divine
ear's helm.
Barefoot on the canvas of eternity, she
pours out celestial ink,
Inscribing stories of love and hope, making
weary hearts link.
As the Sun waits to cloak the Earth in
radiant shine,
The dancing spirit savors the heavenly
serenity divine.
Shadows dance with her in silent applause
of her existence,
An endless spectacle of her enchanting
dance persistence.

Her hymn fills the universe with cosmic echo,
Transcending boundaries, wherever the gentle winds blow.
Underneath the silver sprinkles of the cosmic dance floor,
Her soul, her essence, intertwined with the lore.
Dancing barefoot, on the vast stage of creation,
Every beat, every twirl, an ode to divine exhilaration.
Her rhythmic tapestry binds the Universe's heartbeat,
As she transcends, her tale continues, a celestial feat.
An aria of cosmic delight echoes in the sapphire sky,
The spiritual dance continues, as the stars blush with sigh.
And in the soft cadence of the cosmic morn,
The dancing spirit fades, only to be reborn.

# Medicine Wheel

In the ancient realm where spirits dwell,
Upon a timeless plane, pure and serene,
In silence sits the sacred Medicine Wheel,
A celestial instrument, divine and unseen.
Four directions it honors, symbolically
aligned,
To North, East, South, and West, it pays
heed,
An ode to nature's elements, beautifully
designed,
For our hearts to follow, for our souls to
lead.
North reflects winter, with lessons of
endurance,
East signifies rebirth in the warm light of
spring,
South echoes the vibrance of summer's
essence,
West embodies autumn and the
transformations it brings.
On this eternal compass, spirits humbly
commune,

Life, death, rebirth, in its ethereal spool
spun.
Bridging Earth and Cosmos, a symbolic
tune,
A cosmic map, connecting the Moon, the
Earth, the Sun.
Bearing colors of creation, lessons for every
life stage,
The sacred circle represents healing, unity,
perfection,
Revering the animal totems, the wise elders
engage,
Teaching ancient wisdom, sparking inner
reflection.
We trace its infinite circle, its celestial blend,
Where starts and ends merge in timeless
lore,
Where all paths converge, where all
journeys end,
Within the Medicine Wheel, forever to
explore.
Invoking visions, invoking dreams,
A silent whisper on the universal stream,
We are guided by its spectral beams,
An eternal dance in the cosmic scheme.

Oh Medicine Wheel, timeless and transcendent,
With each spin, a silent hymn of spiritual elation,
You bridge realms, healing and evident,
An embodiment of love, life, and creation.
A map to our inner cosmos, a beacon of pure light,
Guiding us on our spiritual journey, beyond earthly sight,
Within its circle, we find wisdom and might,
Bearing the truths of the universe, beautiful and bright.

## *Animal Totems*

Upon the tranquil land they rest,
silent symbols manifest,
From earthly to ethereal realm,
spiritual guides at the helm.
Each bearing wisdom from ancient roots,
their mysteries unfold like cryptic suits.
Bear totem strong and kind,
draws courage forth from body and mind,
Wolf of twilight's veil so fine,
a pack leader and a spirit divine.
Mighty eagle soars in open sky,
lends vision, freedom, to heart and eye.
Mystic dolphin, an aquatic dream,
immersed in deep thoughts' blue-stream,
With echoes from the fathomless ocean,
scribe of boundless emotion.
From cat's sacred mystique,
whispers of mystery they leak.
The swift fox reveals the way,
while snake uncoils the secrets of the day.
And the great wise old owl sings,
its notes healing what life stings.
Dragonfly embodies our inner light,

with fluttering wings glowing bright.
Oh, hummingbird so joyous, yet slight,
in each nectar there's love's delight.
Spider's web links our space and time,
to grasp all is divine,
Whilst mystical raven reigns in nighttime
skies,
eyes open, always wise.
Animal totems whisper life's endless truth,
resonating through a primal flute.
Their medicine touches heart and soul,
weaves patterns in the celestial scroll.
Spirits of land, sky, and sea,
connect us to nature's reverie.
As we honor their profound link,
wisdom grows with each symbolic ink.
Thus, may we hear their whispered tales,
carried to us on mystic gales.
In earthly bodies, we learn to feel,
the spiritual power they gently reveal.

## Age of Obsession

In this age of obsession, with vanities vast,
As people of Earth our possessions amass.
From tiny trinkets to houses so grand,
But what value carries in God's Holy Land?
Lusting for jewels, yearning for gold,
Have we forgotten the tales of old?
Where virtue was cherished, wisdom
revered,
Has this generation's spiritual sight cleared?
Bound by our shackles of material gain,
Burning within us, an unending flame.
We hunger and thirst, more is our plea,
Ignoring the Truth, that the soul must be
free.
Look at the lilies, the birds of the air,
No worldly concerns do these creatures
bear.
Serving their purpose, so humble and small,
In Its creation, they echo God's call.
In Its wide heavens, amidst stars
uncounted,

On Its grand earth, with creatures surrounded,
A jewel more precious, a treasure unseen,
The divine spark within, obscured by our sheen.
Shatter these shackles, unbind these chains,
To chase fleeting pleasure, invites lasting pains.
Let's sow the seeds of spiritual thought,
Watered by wisdom, the elders had taught.
Delve within the Self, seek out your Soul,
Discover that Love, can make you whole.
Find not your worth in trinkets or gold,
But in kindness and virtue, as the tales of old.
Turn your heart towards the divine,
Find peace in prayer, let Love light shine.
In stillness listen, to the whispering breeze,
Its love in creation, Its order in seas.
In this age of obsession, may we remember,
To seek first the kingdom, a heavenly splendor.
The grandeur of God, within every grain,
To honor, to serve, to love in Its name.

Its Grace transcends, our treasures on Earth,
This Truth eternal, is of infinite worth.
To live by faith, hope, love – that's our mission,
A noble endeavor, in this age of obsession.

# Age of Oppression

Beneath the greyed skies of trials, amidst the storm of oppressions,
Rises a song of courage, of valor against depressions.
The age of oppression has arrived, like a thief in the quietest night,
But every soul will persist and struggle, clad in resolute might.
We walk in shadows of deceit, pierced by blades of ingratitude,
In search of justice, faith, and freedom - things lost in servitude.
Yet from our souls, now strengthened by trial, radiates a divine light,
Exposing the lies, unearthing truths, fighting with holy might.
God, give us the strength to conquer fear, bless us with resilience,
Wrap us in courage to defy the dark, bolster our endurance.
The Age of Oppression tries to erode the bedrock of our faith,

Yet we stand firm, heart ablaze with resolve,
facing wrath's strait.
We sing not of despair and grief, but
resilience in adversity,
Praising our God, whose love we wear as
our invisible armory.
Raising our voices to the Heavens above,
declaring God's renown,
In Its refuge, we find fortitude, till the
oppression is worn down.
So rise, O children of faith, rise in courage,
in unity, in love,
And lift your voices in celestial song,
reaching to skies above.
In unity, we break the shackles, tear the veil
of darkness apart,
Glowing like stars in the vast expanse,
emblems of a faithful heart.
Yes, the Age of Oppression seeks to
ensnare, to tether our spirit's flight,
Yet we dance in the rhythm of divine
melody, resplendent in God's light.
Bathing in the cascade of grace, flowing
from the Holy Throne,

We fear no oppression, endure all pain, for we are never alone.
For within every soul that trudges through this bitter Age of oppression,
Burns the holy flame of resilience, glowing with God's affection.
And even as night stretches ahead, our faith keeps shining bright,
Illuminating the path, pushing back despair, our beacon in the night.
So let it be known across the land, echoed in each incantation,
God's love and strength prevail eternally, transcending all oppression.
Its glory shines in our hearts so deep, within each reverberation,
Love and faith outlive all trials, defying the Age of Oppression.